Ꮆ

You can mₐ ... ...
through your unique lens of awareness, through your
identity, and discover an insight.

BonBons—The Recipe, pg. 145

We have tried the great new idea, theory, solution
and nothing happened. Our hope, which does indeed
spring eternal, is tuckered out from so much eternal
springing.

A Way to Live, pg. 51

"Too good to be true" is a tug of war between hope
and logic.

Ode to Being "Had," pg. 91

It is children who can raise us, if we can abandon
the notion that we raise them.

Gravity is Heavy, pg. 95

You graduate from intelligence to judgment to wisdom,
but there is something beyond wisdom.

Beyond Knowledge, pg. 64

Desire without effort is dreaming.

Strike Out the Half-Hearted, pg. 55

Art is in us, in our ability to notice.

Art, Music and Beauty, pg. 35

Inner work is the difficult but solitary effort to "take
your invisible mental clothes off" and see yourself
naked and undistorted.

Inner Work, pg. 31

It is not the information that is sent, but what is received that determines communication.

Bring Down the Drawbridge, pg. 11

You reverse the frenzied pressures each moment that you take the time to enjoy or reflect.

Busy, Busy, Busy, pg. 110

We do not acknowledge truth simply by our acceptance or acquiescence, but through our unceasing discovery and application of it.

Fresh Truth, pg. 16

The ability to take advice is superior to the ability to give it.

Advice, Who Needs It? pg. 27

Carve out time and areas in your life where the "right way" or the rational way have no influence.

Jailbreak, pg. 10

Often the achievement of the vision is less important than the way it animates and makes purposeful all the other parts of your life.

Designated Driver, pg. 113

Courage exists when your resolve triumphs over intelligence in the face of self-doubt.

Courage, pg. 13

Fears become stronger as you avoid them. But grappling with them strengthens you while weakening them.

Ship Ahoy, pg. 21

BLOGS by Larry James
CelebrateLove.wordpress.com
CelebrateIntimateWeddings.wordpress.com
NetworkingHQ.wordpress.com

Business Networking HQ
TenCommitmentsofNetworking.com

BonBons
To Sweeten
Your Daily Life

Wisdom that Works!

DR. LYNELLA GRANT

Larry You know how to make BonBons & will never be without. Lynella 1996

The contents of this box contain no calories, but will nourish your mind and spirit. Savor and enjoy. Nibble in any order that suits you.

Warning: When consumed, the contents of this book have the power to change your life!

BonBons
To Sweeten
Your Daily Life

Wisdom that Works!

DR. LYNELLA GRANT

Preface by Cavett Robert

Off the Page
PRESS

Scottsdale, Arizona

BonBons to Sweeten Your Daily Life: Wisdom that Works!

Copyright ©1996 Lynella Grant
ISBN 1-888739-05-3

Publisher: Off the Page Press
P.O. Box 1269, Scottsdale AZ 85251
(602) 874-0050

Library of Congress Cataloging-in-Publication Data
Grant, Lynella, 1944-
    BonBons to sweeten your daily life : wisdom that works /
Lynella Grant : preface by Cavett Robert
        p.   cm.
    Includes index.
    ISBN 1-888739-05-3
    1. Conduct of life.   2. Life skills.   I. Title.
BJ1581.G713   1996
158'.1—DC20   96-2785
                                                            CIP

Cover Photograph
Elliot Lincus, Camel Studios
Phoenix, Arizona

Illustrations
Nick Newberry
Maryanne Gonko

Book Design & Typesetting
SageBrush Publications
Tempe, Arizona

Cover Design
Linda Strauss Advertising
& Running Changes
Phoenix, Arizona

Contents

Treat yourself to a candy.
Sample one, try another, reflect.
This is YOUR box of BonBons.
Enjoy it!

Introduction

CHOCOLATES!!

For me?

Ooooh! They look so good I could eat the whole box!

Let's see now—where should I start?

Every box of chocolate BonBons comes as a treat and a choice. Which kind to eat first? How many do I dare to have now? Do I have to share?

The answers should all be "Suit yourself—whatever you like!"

Consider this book your special box of chocolate BonBons. Open it, then consume as much as you desire, whenever you desire. Eat one; eat several. They are rich enough that you probably can't eat them all in one sitting. Some may take some chewing. As with the best candy, savor it; enjoy it; linger over it. It's all a matter of your personal taste.

For the health conscious, these are calorie-free, cholesterol free, and won't give you zits or melt in the hot car. They will, however, energize and enliven you mentally, emotionally and spiritually. Reading them helps you notice much that is special in your everyday world. Enjoy them all you want—share if you like. . .

The box will never be empty, and neither will your life.

Dedication

To My Mother,

Who lived on the Alaskan frontier and taught me to find and explore the frontiers which can be discovered within each moment.

Acknowledgment

A book like this is the product of a wide array of life experiences. Some BonBons arose through interactions shared with others. It would be impossible to name all the individuals who have influenced the contents. However, I feel it an honor to specifically acknowledge the influence of my long-term mentor, Mary Watt, on my life view, my character and the contents of many of the topics in this book.

Preface

Of all the books I've read in my lifetime, I've never read one so full of creative ideas presented in both a powerful and entertaining way. For instance, who ever heard of the Drawbridge of Life, lowered for the treasures we attract and drawn to prevent those things which do not enrich our future? No one can deny that life is far happier if we learn to *dissolve* our problems rather than struggle through the hazardous process where we attempt to solve them. The author of this great book gives answers to this transition in a clear way, all with the divinity of simplicity.

If you carefully consider the ideas of this book, you will find it more than a learning process; it is a treasured experience. You will live more fully, more effectively and more happily by applying and living the eternal jewels of this great book. What can be a greater benefit to the reader?

I have known Lynella Grant for a long time and I treasure the experience. She lives the same way she writes. She demonstrates through daily activities that she is a model of what she writes about.

Cavett Robert
Phoenix, Arizona

Note to the Politically Correct

I refer to anyone or everyone without regard to gender, race, religion, age or politics, since I think being human is more general and important than any such classifications. Therefore, I may offend some readers with the less "correct" term. Please see past my lapses and catch my point—it could apply to you.

I think EVERYONE is special, so I do not relate to redress, revenge, or victimization. All of those who have discovered their own specialness will not be stopped by limiting conditions, even when they are truly present.

Chapter 1

Creams

Trust Yourself and You Won't Get Creamed

Where do you place your confidence? Where do you turn for support, for strength—to others or to yourself? What always comes through for you?

Self-reliance develops along with an awareness of your own deep strengths. Yet, without direct and sustained contact with your solid strengths, you are vulnerable to your every change of mind, and every change of heart. In order to trust yourself you must first KNOW yourself, then VALUE yourself, and finally RESPECT yourself. You're worth all the effort required, for it can truly be said about your relationship with yourself, "'til death do you part."

Each BonBon is a treat and reminder. Trusting yourself brings extra rewards.

Jailbreak

Logic is a jailer. It keeps us functioning with preset limits and punishes us for escaping. It constructs restrictive and confining mental structures more solid than brick and mortar. Try spending a little bit of time every day eluding it. Carve out time and areas in your life where the "right way" or the rational way have no influence. Find lots of "wrong," awkward, silly, irrational ways to do the most familiar things.

Logic is over-rated. There are a zillion things in which it is not helpful at all. And it is so seldom fun. Abandoning it is often fun and fraught with surprises. So take a holiday from your intellect, first in small doses or activities. Then let the freedom creep into more and more of what you do. Break out of your own routine. Sure, you'll be "back to normal" soon enough.

Fear not, you can always get back and reclaim your briefly abandoned mental structure. But like any holiday, you return with fresh insights, a renewed and broadened awareness. You return with added flexibility, aware of more choices, even within your familiar limitations.

Back to jail? Maybe, but is it really a prison when you hold the key? Or does it become a prison only because you fail to use your key?

Bring Down the Drawbridge

Our attention is courted by thousands of suitors every day. Every person, every product, every activity we encounter stakes a claim on our attention, on our time. Yet, at each moment, whenever we notice one thing we fail to respond to the rest. The demands on our attention are so great, we have to be selective—to respond only to those things which capture our interest.

Our minds are like a well-fortified castle. When we are threatened or uninterested we pull up the drawbridge. We withdraw. Only something of interest can make us bring the drawbridge back down. Much of what passes for communication occurs while one or both people are locked within their closed-up mental castles. No information can be transferred when the drawbridge is up. It is not the information that is sent, but what is *received* that determines communication. We get both drawbridges down only when both parties are open to each other.

Each of us needs to invest the time and trust to get the other person's drawbridge down *before* we send our message. It is important that we continue to speak in ways that do not make the other person withdraw their open bridge. To sustain real communication, we must continue to re-establish trust and shared areas of interest. It is worth the trouble. Otherwise, we end up only speaking to ourselves.

Courage

Courage is very private and very lonely. Although courage is seen as the stuff of greatness, you do not feel great when confronted with a need for courage. Far from it. The need for greatest courage comes precisely at the time when you are most aware of your limitations, your sense of powerlessness, and your unpalatable options in the face of overpowering difficulty. At that point, it takes enormous courage to go forth boldly and willingly to confront the Hydra (many-headed beast).

Perhaps the monster cannot be defeated. Perhaps you are wise to avoid the unwinnable battle. Yet to yield to the reluctance to stand firm denies the silent strength that arises only in the face of such difficulties. When you pit yourself against a great challenge, you are forced to take your measure. And you seldom feel that you "measure up" in your own eyes. It takes courage to confront the threat when you "know" yourself to be insufficient to the task. Yet you resolve to do your best, or what little you can do, *anyway*.

Courage exists when your determination triumphs over intelligence in the face of self-doubt. The effort you make in the face of overwhelming odds is your true victory. You may fail, yet you can't be a failure because you tried. You may succeed against all odds and feel triumphant. The point to remember is, the outcome does not validate or diminish your courage. Your WILLINGNESS to proceed *anyway* is the true hallmark of courage.

Chapter 1

Every day each of us encounters situations that call on us to act courageously. To live fully challenges us to frequent acts of courage, but it's up to us to make that choice. The first act of courage is the willingness to act with courage.

Other People

There are a lot of "other people" out there. Some we know, some we don't, but they all influence us somehow, intentionally or unintentionally. How we look at ourselves determines the extent to which the faceless "other people" control us.

It is human nature to have a lot of misperceptions about ourselves. They are not easy to overcome. You have to sort them out carefully to define who you are. Until you bother to discover and develop your own personal strengths and values, you don't know what YOU think about something. Does your opinion reveal or obscure who you are? Is that opinion compatible with your strongest beliefs? Sincerely-held opinions require strength—they also build strength. While it is O.K. to change opinions, it should be done without discarding either your underlying value system or your sense of personal identity. Only when you have invested the effort to become aware of your unique identity and have invested the effort to establish your opinions, will "other people" cease to control what you think.

Fresh Truth

Truth can too easily become a cliché. The old truths that we've heard or spoken over and over gradually degrade into dogma. As it eventually becomes rigid, it is less capable of discerning or responding to subtle nuances. Such truth is wielded like a sword—stiff, unbending, heavy-handed. Certainly, the words are still true, but much of the force that made them relevant has been lost. The effort to sustain such heavy truth stifles both you and the truth you value.

Despite our most sincere efforts, such truths cannot inspire or be living forces to animate the way we make decisions. We need to discover truth and continually rediscover truth for it to remain live and relevant to us. The desire to find and then to express the truth is ACTIVE. It demands much more than a passive parroting of slogans. We do not acknowledge truth simply by our acceptance or acquiescence, but through our unceasing discovery and application of it.

The awareness of freshly rediscovered truth has force. It animates. It uplifts. It resonates through whatever we are doing. New-found truth is not simply true, but through us it becomes alive and true. In such ways we can renew truth and make it a vital force. Truth cannot exist in a static state; unless it is renewed, it hardens or withers. When it is not fresh truth, it becomes less than true.

Energy Policies

Politicians have it all wrong. They think that the country needs energy use and conservation policies dealing with oil, gas and nuclear energy. The energy policy that is needed most is the one each of us develops for ourselves. Where do we get our energy and how can we get more of it, so we can face each day with enthusiasm and force?

Next, notice where the energy goes. What saps our spirit leaving us drained and discouraged? Energy can leak away, like water draining through holes in the plumbing. Then, no matter how much we start with, it is soon gone. We end up feeling stranded and depleted. Those leaks are the places where we need to make repairs.

As we work on our personal energy priorities, we discover ways to make adjustments, much like a well-trained mechanic. Soon we have our lives running like a tuned-up automobile. Then we can go wherever we want—with energy to spare.

Right Here Is the Right Place*

I am in the right place to make a very important difference in my life and in the lives of those around me. No one else can make this difference. It is my unique opportunity. If I fail to make an adequate effort, an irreplaceable opportunity is lost. The choice is mine to make, and is re-offered all day long. The endeavor permits me to participate fully in my life, in my milieu. All that is required of me is a sincere desire to accept and use the opportunities my life lays before me.

*and right now is the right time

Treasure Hunt

Socrates was right. We already have the answers built into our minds. Unfortunately, there is just so much junk in there too, that it's impossible to tell which things to use, which things to trust, which things to discard. It's very difficult to sort it out, while more information is dumped in all the time.

It makes good sense to avoid the old stuff in there, like a moldy attic, and go look for "new" better answers—hence the quest for fresh sure-fire ideas and easy remedies. Fads emerge and fade to be replaced by newer, flashier, up-to-the-minute notions that don't work any better than the recently-abandoned fads of last year. That's what popular culture demands—and delivers. Anyone with the desire to find an answer to life's serious, or even frivolous, questions gets sucked into the process.

Let us pause to notice that *all* those fads lead us to seek answers "out there" from other people. The quicker and more painless the results promised, the more eager we become. Eventually, we become disillusioned, without ever securing the answers we seek. All those quests blind us to the fact that we already KNOW the answers we need (that is not the same as saying we have all the information there is). Such answers are simple and trustworthy, buried under years of accumulated "knowledge." We have to dig INSIDE ourselves to find them, and keep digging to find the entire treasure. But it's there.

From time to time, we'll hear or read a statement to which we respond almost wistfully, "I already knew that . . . but I'd forgotten." We must reclaim and embrace that truth, because for that moment each of us discovers afresh that we have our own answers WITHIN, as well as the ability to recognize them. Those carefully-garnered chunks of reclaimed truth are ours to use and provide a reliable foundation for living an entire life.

So, go sorting in the attic. Spend some time up there. Find your own buried treasures in all that jumble. Use and display them like proud family heirlooms. Cast out some of the debris. Your mind will richly reward you as you resurrect that long-hidden horde. You already have your treasure; go claim it.

Ship Ahoy

It was always my greatest fear that when the time of severe testing or significant opportunity came, I would miss the boat. I feared that my own lack of attention, preparation or desire would waste the long-awaited opportunity. I have since come to realize that I am ALREADY doing my life's work and fulfilling my destiny. Instead of "missing the boat," I'm aboard and launched. I had doubted that I would be prepared, but my mission is already occurring.

How easily our fears can blind and mislead us. Mine compelled me to push myself relentlessly to cultivate my strengths and confront my weaknesses. Such efforts occupied me so fully, that I failed to notice that my initial fear was no longer valid. Nevertheless, it had served me as a worthy impetus for self-growth.

Fear is only good when you *use* it. Grab it and struggle against it. It will make you potent. Fears become stronger as you avoid them. But grappling with them strengthens you while weakening them. What an irony! What an obscured truth!

Don't Kill the Song

There was a beautiful bird that flew into a high-walled garden. The bird would sing wondrous songs, unlike any that had been heard before. But it was not just the melodies that made these songs special; everyone who listened felt stronger. They felt they had whatever was needed to reach their heart's desire. When the bird would sing, they felt a longing to do whatever was necessary to accomplish their dreams.

The bird would eat the berries from only one bush in the garden. One day someone complained: "Why do we let the bird eat those berries? There won't be enough left for us." Then, whenever the bird approached the bush it was shooed away. After the first day, it stopped singing and very soon it flew away.

Those who had felt strong enough to achieve their dreams began to have doubts. They forgot a greater vision. Before long what had been a heart's desire became only a fading dream.

MORAL: Value and encourage those things which help you develop and sustain your vision. They are fragile and fleeting.

Who's Dreaming
the American Dream?

I remember when everyone I knew wanted to grow up and be president or do something great (be an astronaut, find a cure for cancer) or make something creative like an invention or the next "hula hoop." We were eager to make our mark by showing the world what we could do. We wanted to be rich and famous, confident we'd do something worthwhile. Sure, we expected it to be hard work—you had to stick your neck out and hang on through "hell and high water." But in the end, we'd triumph because we'd stuck to it, and the world rewarded those who refused to be defeated. That was the American dream, as I remember it. Work hard to achieve your dream, get smarter, pay the price in blood and hard work, and you would achieve the good life.

Nowadays, that is not the prevailing view. People still want to be rich and famous, but not with all that demanding effort. Instead, wealth is seen as random, showered on us not because we're so capable, but because we "got lucky." We expect the lottery or some other random event to change our lives, instead of trusting our own struggling creative efforts. Our success resides in forces we can't control rather than in our own hands. Forces from outside, rather than within us determine success.

Our Constitution guarantees the "pursuit of happiness"—but it recognizes you have to PURSUE IT! There

are no assurances beyond those you can secure your-
self. So define the dream you want to ardently and
relentlessly pursue. Make it a top priority. Steadfastly
devote yourself to fulfilling that dream. Only then will
you stop dreaming and see that you're already LIVING
YOUR OWN American dream.

My Holiday

When I was still in high school I started setting aside one particular day a year to take stock of my life. On that day I am never available to anyone for any reason ("She is having her day off."). I withdraw to figure out where I am in my life: what's working, what isn't, what hurts, what is "out of whack," in addition to taking notice of the good parts. The day is devoted to unbridled ruthlessness and candor (no delusions permitted). I take notes, probe what feels tender, critique my behavior, then scrutinize my goals and how well I'm achieving them. All parts of my life are "on the table," open to re-evaluation.

By noon, my brutal honesty has brought tears, since my ego has taken some direct, well-aimed hits. But, they are cleansing tears, which clear my vision and permit me to see myself anew. As the old is purged, understood and forgiven, I am left feeling empty.

The early part of the day is always similar—painfully draining, but fundamentally purifying. Once I become totally and deeply empty, I lose any idea of which direction to go. What can take the place of the pieces that are now gone? My mind is at a loss, yet I earnestly, passionately NEED answers. This phase requires that I stay open to my higher nature, while resisting any preference for the form the answers will take.

I wander about (indoors and out), letting my attention grab where it will: flip through a book, listen to music, take a walk. It seems so aimless, and it is hard to remain patient and receptive. By late afternoon a word comes, an idea emerges, an image lingers. I hold . . . waiting . . . watching . . . listening . . . Eventually, with clarity, I begin to see afresh my own over-arching purpose and goals. Gradually the "hows" start falling into place. My priorities start to become obvious; logical steps and pieces fit together as parts of a coherent picture. What a relief!

Each year I doubt that it can work this time. Each year the process creates a vacuum whereby I discover anew my own deeper hidden wisdom. By the end of the incredibly intense day, when I re-dedicate myself to the re-awakened vision, I am both humbled and confident. I have a plan and total commitment to it that charges me and everything that happens with fresh meaning.

The date of my holiday is always the fourth day of March. After the day of discovery and renewal it serves as my mandate: MARCH FORTH!

Advice, Who Needs It?

Advice can be the most valuable or most worthless thing in the world. So how can anyone tell? You probably can't tell which is good advice. Anyone who is able to tell the difference, probably doesn't need the advice anyway. Besides, the ability to take advice is superior to the ability to give it. The worth of the advice can only be determined later—by what has been done with it, by what develops because of it. And that brings in a lot of other factors beyond the value of the information.

Not all advice is distilled wisdom. Every bit of it reflects the values and philosophy of the advice giver. All of it relates to a particular time, place and circumstance and may not work in other settings.

Seldom is advice treated as communication, with a two-way dialogue. Usually, there is a giver and a receiver, an inherent inequality which implies one person knows and the other doesn't. More likely, both of them know partially and through a shared effort both could know and accomplish more. The giver and receiver should focus less on the advice than on the sharing experience. The times when advice is transmitted can become the source of new awareness, of synergy, when both the giver and receiver end up being better informed.

It cannot be denied that the best advice is a good example. Our acts are much more potent and persuasive than anything that comes from our mouths.

Into the Fray

We have entered a period with very few answers yet many things that do not work well: our economy, with its trade imbalance abroad and declining standards at home; education, which cannot consistently deliver an employable graduate; the family, which is no longer a primary force for instilling values and stability; government, which is incapable of responsible leadership. Commentators are unsure what to name this period, but I suggest the Era of Befuddlement. At every level of society, our desires are thwarted, leaving us to feel puzzled, disappointed and impotent.

Isn't the cavalry coming to the rescue? Surprise, IT'S YOU! You are the salvation you've clamored for. Except for what you are willing to do, there is no cavalry.

Visualize yourself as a soldier, armed only with your determination, which feels as frail as a hatpin against a sword. Scary? Of course! Your best hope is to attack each menace while it is small and near at hand, while it still underestimates you. Strike those intimidating perils at each point they impact upon you. Take a stand on small issues, using your clearly focused hatpin against their tiny vulnerabilities. Resist impending threats, confident only that you'll do your best. You'll be amazed to discover what one person with perseverance can achieve. This process transforms an ordinary person into the kind of leader we admire.

Chapter 2

Fudge
Effective Living
(No Fudging)

We experience life on parallel tracks:

What we WANT to happen
What we THINK is happening
What REALLY is happening
What COULD BE happening, here and now

When these views all converge and match we are our most effective and happy. The more they diverge, the more they are different from each other, the more miserable we become. As we know and accept ourselves, these differences diminish. As our awareness and intensity of desire increase, we can find new ways to bring them closer together. We gain a sharper focus. Then we can live ever more effectively, joyously and energetically. Then we simultaneously discover and reveal our true identity through every action we take.

These BonBons will nurture you while you pursue your quest for a fully satisfying life.

My Life Matters

My life matters; and because I know that, everything I do matters. I have a responsibility to prefer the worth-while above the superficial and make the choices which reflect that I can tell the difference. In each little activity of the day, it is possible to discover that there is meaning and there is a meaningful choice to be made. The more I discover and seek out that truth, the more I learn that NOTHING I do is insignificant.

Inner Work

Inner work is hard work.

It is not daydreaming.

It is not introspection.

It is not wishful thinking.

It is not dogma or beliefs.

It is not creative visualization.

It is not self-judgment or criticism.

Inner work is learning about yourself from the INSIDE. It reveals to you what works for you and what doesn't. You begin to see your limits with candor and acceptance. You find and repair damaged and hurt places. You discover strengths and virtues you didn't know you had. Your goal is not to change, but to truly understand yourself, as you *already* are.

Too often, people are not satisfied with themselves and spend considerable effort trying to change into being someone they would like better. Those efforts to change are very different from what is required to know yourself. Yet, attempts to change are doomed unless they include an awareness of what is already in operation. The better way to grow is to value those qualities which are already functioning and enhance them. Then you are building on your strengths, using your resources to greater advantage.

Inner work is the difficult but solitary effort to "take your invisible mental clothes off" and see yourself naked and undistorted. As you eliminate all pretense, all muddled thinking, all preconceptions, you see your own real self—honestly and with love. The combination of courage, vulnerability, trust and gentleness necessary to "Know yourself" is hard to achieve. But inner work cannot occur without them.

Eight-Foot Pigmy

Once in a while I get jolted from my everyday mind-set. Then I look about and say to myself, "Where have I been?!! Why have I been out of touch with this?" I am able to see everything with fresh eyes and clarity. It's much better than being emotionally "up" or having a good day. I feel taller, straighter, infinitely capable, unflappable, joyous, full of goodwill, focused and energized. It always feels like it will last forever, never to be lost again. That's what I call being an EIGHT-FOOT PIGMY.

Whenever you're lost in the little demands and pressures of life and find yourself tossed about, being glad just to hang on, you're being a Four-Foot Pigmy. It's possible to muddle along like that for a long time without any doubt that that is all there is.

An Eight-Foot Pigmy knows he's *not* a Four-Foot Pigmy—at the moment. But he also knows it is possible (even likely) to return to being one again. The Eight-Foot Pigmy also knows that he must do whatever possible as quickly as possible to break the links (habits) that tie him to being the Four-Foot Pigmy. It is URGENT! These are the bridges that need burning. The Eight-Foot Pigmy senses the urgency of doing everything possible to sustain that perspective: find other Eight-Foot Pigmies (there are others), read powerful books, jettison unproductive activities, make fresh supportive commitments. Change is easy when you're tall, yet barely thinkable when you're shrunken.

Oh yes, we've all been in both modes, and each of them feels real while we're in it. So, which mode are you pursuing? How tall does it make you feel? Aspire to be the Eight-Foot Pigmy, even when it eludes you. Treasure your life and those around you. Select life-enhancing pursuits whenever you can. Acting like you're an Eight-Foot Pigmy already is likely to assure that it comes true.

Art, Music and Beauty

Art and music are about beauty. They have to do
with the way we experience our world—not as some-
thing isolated and set down by the masters in the great
classics. We turn our attention to the colors of the
evening sky, the subtle shades and shadows of a loved
one's face, the silhouette of a bird perched on a light
pole. We hear the music in the sounds and rhythms of
the falling rain, the laughter and squeals from a play-
ground, the chirping of a cricket.

Art is all around us, and yet it is not the things we
experience. Art is in us—in our ability to notice. An
eye or an ear tuned to lovely things will always be
surrounded by them. The more that we have the urge
to notice, the more power beauty will have to touch
our lives.

Feel Good Multiplier

Next time someone says or does something that:

a) Makes you feel better

b) Went the extra mile for you

c) Exceeded your expectations

Resolve to do that very same thing to the next ten people who could benefit from the same kind of experience.

Forget about whether or not you think they "deserve" it. Look for any opportunity to keep that special feeling alive. Treat it like a chain letter; pass it on right away. Don't break the chain.

Be alert for situations to do it—THEN DO IT! This is a life changer and an energizer—you'll see! You'll get back much more than you send out, and you'll SURE FEEL GOOD.

Fat Head

"I'm too fat," "I've got to diet," "My clothes are too tight," "I'm eating too much," or even "I'm too thin." Such recurring mental chatter has a way of creeping in throughout other activities. It colors the enjoyment of many things other than food: our friendships, our job, our leisure activities. It tears at our self-confidence and redefines our self-image.

Yet, the solution is not primarily related to what to eat—or even how much to eat. Changing eating habits, or resolving to change them, would make little real difference. The problem of weight control has less to do with your eating habits than you think. It has less to do with will power than you think. It has less to do with genetic disposition than you think. Each of those, and all the other areas of our ready excuses, are only secondary. So it's no wonder that placing your attention and resolutions on them has so little effect.

Food and the way you relate to it have become TOO CENTRAL in your life. Eating (or not eating) doesn't deserve to be your primary concern. Figure out what you prefer to have as your central concern. Find a guiding passion, a commitment to something you *really* feel strongly about. Put more time and energy there. Find ways to make it central to your daily activities. Invest yourself in that pursuit—think and dream about it.

As something more significant fills your attention, your preoccupation with food or your weight recedes. It then takes its proper place in your life. Once food ceases to have an over-riding influence, you can enjoy it and stop treating it as a stick you use to beat yourself.

A Good Attitude Stinks

You CANNOT get through life on a good attitude.

What you need is instead an attitude that is good—one that brings you joy.

A good attitude is better than a bad attitude, but that's about all. Although we are often urged to have a good attitude, it is not a good thing; it is a counterfeit of something good. It's what you have settled for *instead* of getting what you really wanted.

A good attitude is based on "I don't like this, but I'll be good about it," or "I'm having a terrible time, but I'll pretend it's O.K." When did you have to have a good attitude about something you *really* enjoyed doing? It's unthinkable!

Enjoyment and a good attitude are opposites. Who could be sincerely pleased about a counterfeit reward? The more things you have a good attitude about, the more things you really don't get to enjoy. So, don't be so proud of having a good attitude—it's not the right answer. It is partly right (bad attitude is also not the right answer), but it's simply not enough.

Whenever you find that you are having a good attitude, recognize it as a clue that "there is something amiss here." Like a determined detective, you must take a closer look; search for other clues. Look with candor and see what it is you don't like. Often it is something that others have imposed on you, like rigid rules or a powerplay. Sometimes, it can't be changed, like the weather or a personal tragedy.

Whatever it is, say to yourself, "Instead of having a good attitude about this, I'm going to find a way to enjoy myself *anyway*. I'm going to find some way, however small, where this situation cannot dictate how I must react. And I'm going to turn it into something positive for myself." That effort shifts you from feeling powerless to gearing up to discover an outcome that would be even better. You have also avoided the smelly trap of a good attitude. Instead, you've demonstrated "an attitude that is good." Notice how totally terrific you feel!

Such detective work is very powerful and satisfying. Once such clues start coming to your attention, there's no telling what else you'll solve—and how good you'll feel, again and again and again!

Treat Your Life Like a Garden

Clear out underbrush; weed out old clutter.

Plant trees; labor over long-term goals.

Plant annuals; pursue short-term projects with lots
of variety, color and fragrance.

Search out new and lovely things for your garden.

Stay vigilant for weeds; watch for early signs of
problems and pull them up by the roots.

Water it, tend it; do some work on it often.

Fertilize it; add whatever is missing.

Establish paths; keep the goals visible and walk
on them.

Sit and enjoy it; savor the sensations.

Each garden is different; each season is different.

Learn to like them all and appreciate their
differences.

Others can enjoy your garden and you can
enjoy theirs.

Give away some flowers; when you do, you always
get more.

Fill the space with things you love.

Tending your garden takes your entire lifetime, but
what else could possibly be more important—or more
enjoyable?

First Aid for Inner Hurts

Science has proven that you cannot feel bad at the same time you're doing something nice for someone else.

Feeling bad is hard work. It consumes a lot of time and energy and usually feeds on old hurts: "This always happens to me," "I hate it when she says that," "I can't handle this."

Everyone gets hurt, whether intentionally or not. You get to decide how much of your life you are willing to invest in thinking about it, ruminating on it, reliving it, protecting yourself from it, grieving about it. It's time to move on. Shift your attention.

Here's a quick and lasting fix: find someone who can benefit from doing something you really enjoy. Do it together without delay. Sharing magnifies the enjoyment and increases your energy. You'll soon forget that you were ever feeling bad.

Reading Rite

Why read faster? Better to reflect, enjoy, ponder the words. Read intently, feeling a direct connection with the writer. Sense what the writer was feeling: all five senses, the complexity of the time and setting, the influence of the characters, the frustrations inherent in the topics. Invest your emotions in the experience, as you are investing your attention. Like any other investment, insist on a return, a payback to justify your time.

Overwhelmed? There's too much to read? Be ruthlessly selective. Demand that the books you read reward you for the time you have invested—or avoid that author henceforth.

Reading faster—pooh! That's like eating faster. It's not about quantity. It's not about pace. It is about taking the time to enjoy an experience fully. That's always worth the effort—don't rush it.

To Forgive Isn't Divine

To forgive a prior grievance has nothing to do with religion. It has to do with whether I choose to let past experiences and old hurts dictate my relationships with those around me today. Whatever happened back then and who did it, or why, are not important now. Even what has happened since then is not important. To forgive simply permits me to drop that old baggage which has been trotted along, limiting my options since then. If I forgive, those heavy burdens are gone. The painful recollections are gone. Only then can I discover that forgiveness has little to do with the other person or with noble sentiments. It is about regaining my own freedom.

So set yourself free. Clear the air by deleting those painful, awkward recollections. Forgive the other person. Forgive yourself. Poof! They're gone, over, finished, kaput.

Rejoice! You're free!

Your Special Calendar

When you rename something that is very familiar, each time you hear or say the word, it will remind you to see whatever you are doing with fresh eyes. These silly variations can act as reminders that even the ordinary things have excitement when you take the time to notice them.

Months of the Year

JANUARY	CAN YOU VARY?—Of course! Add variety.
FEBRUARY	FAB YOU ARE, EH? Aren't you great!
MARCH	MARCH—Go forth! Go for it!
APRIL	A THRILL—Whee! Enjoy it.
MAY	PLAY—Have fun.
JUNE	CROON (your tune)—Sing your *own* song.
JULY	YOU TRY—Then achieve
AUGUST	AWE GUSH—A blast of amazement
SEPTEMBER	STEP MENDER—Fix things and move forward.
OCTOBER	ACT OLDER—Prepare to grow; be wise.
NOVEMBER	NEW VEMBER—All is fresh.
DECEMBER	RE MEMBER—Reflect, relive, renew

Days of the Week

SUNDAY	FUN DAY—Play all day
MONDAY	PUN DAY—Find humor and laughter.
TUESDAY	TWOS DAY—Double the intensity/energy/enjoyment
WEDNESDAY	WINS DAY—You can't lose!
THURSDAY	THIRST DAY—Drink in experiences!
FRIDAY	MY DAY—Claim it! Make it yours.
SATURDAY	GLADDER DAY—Not sadder day

How Many Ways Can You Count to Ten?

1. FUN
2. DO
3. FREE
4. MORE
5. ALIVE
6. TRICKS
7. GROOVIN
8. GREAT
9. MINE
10. AGAIN
20. PLENTY
50. NIFTY
100. UNHINDERED

A Holiday Tradition

Not long ago, I spent Thanksgiving with a friend who had recently married. She was the hostess facing her first holiday feast with her new in-laws and other guests. She was fearful about doing things right, about living up to their expectations, that her cooking skills were inadequate. I told her she only needed to remember one thing: Whatever happens, say, "That's the way we did it at our house."

She created a holiday tradition that day. She was not intimidated by the opinions of the more aggressive guests. At each potentially touchy point, where someone made a face or requested something that was not available, she would beam and announce without apology, they didn't do it that way at her house. No criticism, no subtle preference, no personal one-up-manship counted that day. She sailed confidently through it all, exuding full command, and with tradition as her ally.

Before long it became a game. People would stop themselves from comparisons and say, "I'll bet that's the way you did it at your house." Everyone felt as though they were in on the joke, but it added sparkle and a touch of humor to the eating activities.

She already has a very important tradition in her new home. That's her willingness to say, "That is the way . . ."

Chapter 3

Nuts

Do It!

Ideas are great; actions are greater. Ideals are potent; deeds rooted in ideas are even more powerful. When noble concepts can be mobilized through tangible acts the world notices—and responds.

First we know something with our minds (logic/ ideas). Then we come to know it with our hearts (emotion/values). Later, we reveal that we know through our behavior (deeds/character). There is often a long span of time between the first "knowing" and demonstrating it through our daily activities.

As with any other skill-building, we must try, try, and keep trying in order to become stronger. Sustained efforts DO count. Sometimes, the only rewards along the path to mastery are the little victories experienced in maintaining our resolutions. These candies provide a boost to determination, so we can get out there and DO IT!

Democracy Through Action

We don't just vote at the ballot box. We vote in our daily lives as citizens—for those causes and concerns we believe in and against those things of which we disapprove.

We vote with our time—whether we invest it in cultural or civic activities, or in the movies and TV programs we watch.

We vote with our money—with regard to which products and charities get to receive our patronage.

We vote with our kind and supporting words—to a young person making an effort to learn, to an old person making an effort to stay involved.

We vote with our behavior—whether we drive with safety and with courtesy, or whether we are wasteful.

What happens at the polls or through government affects us a lot less than the frequent votes each one of us gets to cast every day. Make your votes count. Choose the activities which give you pleasure. Cast your ballot for beneficence in your world. See yourself as a citizen of the universe and vote for its survival and betterment with every choice and every activity. In this way democracy becomes a living force, with you choosing the world you want to live in. You have the power to improve whatever you touch, so why not vote for it?

A Way to Live

The world is full of beautiful ideas, profound philosophies, worthwhile goals. On an even more down-to-earth level, it's full of good advice, as well as a lot of people eager to give it. We are bombarded by great ideas and tempted by dreams of untapped potential, all waiting to be released in our lives. Who could resist endless opportunities that promise to eliminate any problem known to man? As we all know, there is no shortage of motivational rhetoric, but somehow it fails to motivate. Even when we agree and then embrace a worthwhile idea, it seldom has the power to help us solve our daily dilemmas.

I do not think most people are unmotivated or jaded by new ideas. I think that, instead, we are disappointed. We have tried the great new idea, theory, solution and nothing happened. Our hope, which does indeed spring eternal, is tuckered out from so much eternal springing.

Years ago, I encountered a yardstick against which I measure each new notion, my own as well as someone else's. I continue to ask: "Is this a 'way to live?'"

Can I live with more joy and satisfaction by applying this idea? Can it be helpful in my practical daily activities? Is it compatible with my other beliefs? Will it be a benefit to those who are around me? Will I be willing to make the sacrifices or adjustments necessary to make this a functional part of my behavior? If any idea can't measure up by my "way to live" yardstick, I put it aside. It may be a great notion, but it's not for me, at least not now.

I don't just look at the idea itself, I consider how it fits into my life, into my world, into my values. Only then do I "buy it." It is folly to embrace an idea unless it's going to be used, so BUY IT means TRY IT.

Even the grandest concept is of little value until it is put into practice. Any worthy concept that is practiced, even a little bit, is a source of strength and continued rewards. I think of any "way to live" notion that is being translated into behavior by someone as a solid gold nugget, since they surely represent life's greatest treasures. I am forever on the lookout for those clear notions that can touch me enough to stand as a "way to live" day by day. Each such nugget has made me feel a little taller, a little more human, a little less passive, a little more mature.

Such nuggets are very personal because some suit us better than others. Each of us must choose those that speak to our sincere desires in life. We can seek out additional messages in daily activities, for they are always there to be found. Anyone with the determination to find their nuggets will end up with their own pot of gold!

I Could Do Better

"I could do better" are wonderfully dangerous words because once you've said them, you begin to see all sorts of ways to make them true. Once you act on them, they lead you in directions you could never have planned to go. They lead you to develop unrecognized strengths, while abandoning areas of weakness.

"I could do better" does not criticize what is already happening. Rather, it turns the attention toward what more is possible: more efficient, more beautiful, more economical, more enjoyable, more wholesome, more useful. First you envision creatively. Then you harness all resources and figure out how to get it done.

I said those words some years ago after being involved in several family matters involving attorneys. The next thing I knew, I was in law school. Later, once I was in private practice, I used those words as my guide to see that each client got the best service I could provide.

Uttering those words evokes continuous lifelong growth. It works on ANYTHING you do: cooking a meal, mowing the lawn, writing a letter, playing with a child. Even a dull, familiar job becomes enhanced if you're looking for ways to do so. EVERYTHING becomes a challenging task for you. You go beyond the way "everybody does it" and make something special. Constantly consider what new element you can add.

Useful inventions or successful enterprises are often the consequence of asking, "How could I do that better?"

Inevitably, the answer comes. Instead of complaining or despairing, look for a remedy or enhancement. Then improve your answer, again and again. You've embarked on a path that can be fun, but never dull!

WARNING: If applied, those words have the power to change everything you do.

Strike Out the Half-Hearted

Whenever confronted with a challenge, it is not enough to want the goal. You also need a vision of what you want. Then you have to commit yourself to dealing with any difficulties encountered along the way. Your dedication helps you mobilize your energy, your drive, and your imagination with enough force to cut through the inevitable obstacles. Few events match our expectations, and seldom will our initial plan be sufficient. Flexibility that is rooted in a willingness to adapt to new information is necessary at each step.

You can be confident of one thing: whatever you anticipate, there will be unexpected difficulties. If you start out half-hearted, you will lack the drive, the energy, the determination to carry on in the face of the escalating demands. Half-hearted efforts can't achieve what you want. Obstacles are inevitable, but they are not what stop you. The real problem is inside, determined by the intensity of your desire and resolve.

Desire without effort is dreaming. It takes a whole-hearted effort to be fully committed to the task.

Half-hearted is half-committed, so what you accomplish will inevitably be half-assed. That's just not good enough. Strike out the half-hearted; strike out the half-assed.

 **=**

Half-Hearted   Is   Half-Assed

Integrity Is Expensive—and Rare

Integrity only applies to behavior—to the way we LIVE our lives. It is not a philosophy so much as a determination that what I say or think is also what I DO. Integrity is very demanding. And it is made even more difficult by the too-human assumption that we're already doing what we intended. Only the shocking discovery of how seldom our words and actions match can compel us to treat it as a serious challenge.

At the point of commitment to the task, our integrity reinforces the determination to avoid self-delusion, superficial answers, or distortions due to wishful thinking. It alone provides the necessary ruthlessness to hold steadfastly to the task (even though the results appear negligible or counter-productive).

Others will not applaud our efforts, even if they notice. But once the resolution is engaged, we learn that each moment requires a rededication to the goal, or the old blind habits will re-assert themselves. The victories are hard-fought, but a new identity is being created. Ah . . . , to be a person of integrity—the rarest kind of human. Yet, each attempt helps to transform us into one.

To Arise Is the Prize

I am not so smart that I cannot make foolish choices.

I am not so strong that I cannot be broken.

I am not so confident that I cannot despair.

I am not so aware that I cannot be fooled.

I am not so determined that I cannot fail.

SO WHAT!

In every case I am willing to try again!

The valor of the effort is not diminished by the outcome.

To try AGAIN, despite disappointment, IS a triumph.

The VALUE of the effort (in this circumstance alone) exceeds the value of the consequences.

He Who Hesitates Is Saved

From time to time each of us gets discouraged. At those times the world seems black and our judgment *cannot* be trusted. While in that mindset, every experience we have is seen as a worst-case scenario. When we are down, we must avoid making decisions—they won't work. That's when we are so frustrated that the urge to DO SOMETHING, no matter what, further fires our sense of frustration. Events seems to say, "Leap—there's no time to look!" with an extreme sense of urgency. Increasing pressures and the demands from other people magnify the unbearable urge for relief. Even when we don't like the possible—or even certain—consequences, they appear less terrible to bear than further endurance now.

Remember, any such urgency is short-lived, no matter how inconceivable that seems at the time. The intensity and passion will cool. The emotional storm which has disrupted all your rational judgment will pass. You will begin thinking clearly again. Wait until then to make ANY choice. Do *not* be fooled by the lie: "You have to decide NOW; you have to DO SOMETHING NOW."

Bide your time, confident that he who hesitates is saved.

Credit Balance

What are you doing about building up your charge accounts? Making steady deposits with puny withdrawals? Is your balance staying in the black or in the red? Do you always struggle against being overdrawn?

Oh, I'm not talking about your finances—but about your energy accounts. They're far more important to you than money, though they seldom get to compete with money for your attention.

Energy provides your life force, the gas that keeps you chugging along. But you can't get far when you try to run on empty. You can try hard, be very motivated and determined, display resolutely focused willpower, yet still be unable to GO. You don't arrive at your destination. The problem may not be in your goal, or your desire or your efforts. Pause and check the gauge— you might just need a fill-up.

Fill up with those things which recharge you, that replenish and gladden you. Don't wait until you're on empty again before you fill back up. Refill at each station, each opportunity. It's amazing how much more mileage and *smile*age you can get on FULL.

Next, notice how you're using up your gas. Are you running around on futile fruitless errands and projects, pursuing those things that bring only discharge, but no recharge? Enough! Stop the withdrawals and increase the deposits. That's the principal (along with compounded interest) that en*RICH*es you and provides for a rewarded future—yours.

You Are What You *DO*

The best idea in the world is of little value if it does not influence how you LIVE your life. Beautiful ideals and ambitious goals are worse than useless trinkets until they are put into practice. Whenever ideals and behavior do not correspond, it is the behavior which reveals the true beliefs. The abstractions are simply providing "lip service."

Any small gesture, kindness, goal that you *act* upon outweighs the grandest philosophies or intentions. Opportunities constantly present themselves: a child stakes a claim on your attention, a clerk obviously having a bad day bungles your order, a thoughtless co-worker offends your sensibility. How do you respond? Will you respond in kind, with indifference, or on the basis of your ideals? For in such exchanges are our true beliefs revealed—to ourselves and the observing world.

We need to stop kidding ourselves about having high ideals unless we can demonstrate them. We only get credit for those notions we USE in our daily living. Practice is never easy and the results are often disappointing. But ONLY such efforts build character and avoid the trap of self-delusion. They also make you a whole lot more pleasant to be around.

Life as the Ultimate Hobby

Every life is a do-it-yourself project. You are issued a standard model—basic equipment (body) with a few variations (gender) and colors (race). You have to care for it, protect it, move it around, decorate it, train it. But most of your important efforts take place on the inside—out of sight in your heart and mind. As you design yourself in your mind, that is what shows on the outside. If you can design the person you admire, you'll be proud of who you are—and it will show. If you don't bother, that too will show. Your design modifications determine the way you live your life and express your unique identity.

Isn't it worth the effort to develop a person you like, that you can enjoy being? You get to experiment and embellish, expand and delete traits or interests as much as you desire. YOU are your hobby, a creative project that is designed to your exacting specifications. It will grow and change as you do. So, throw yourself into it! Give your ultimate hobby all the attention you deserve. And like a cherished hobby, you'll be able to return unlimited satisfaction.

Beyond Knowledge

What you discover from your own experience is more true than anything you can learn from a book (including this one). And that knowledge will become even truer for you if you share the discoveries with other people.

You graduate from intelligence to judgment to wisdom, but there is something beyond wisdom. The bridge from intelligence to judgment is experience. The bridge from judgment to wisdom is character. Yet, wisdom is solitary. Beyond wisdom is generosity of spirit, where wisdom is coupled with the fundamental human need to share and apply what has been learned.

Getting Past the Gates of Avoidance

Sure, you committed, you promised, you fully intended. No question about your resolutions, but somehow, you didn't get around to it. So the next time you felt a bit reluctant, not much, just a smidgen. You still intend to, of course, no question about it, but, oops, it's still on the "to do," open, pending pile.

That's O.K., you're sure to get around to it real soon. But, now it feels awkward, and all the time that has passed reminds you that it should have happened a long time ago. But . . ., though you're not too clear about why, there must have been a good reason . . . Still—no question, you're going to do it.

Only now, it isn't so pressing, somehow. In fact, now that you think about it, it might not be as important as you thought. Now there's a lot of awkwardness whenever you think about it. Might as well avoid thinking about it, for now.

Been there? We all have! The longer we avoid something the more it strengthens our avoidance skills. The more ways we find to fool ourselves. The more mental maneuvers we play—all at the expense of our integrity.

The thing you promised to do may not be that important anymore. It just becomes another example of how your intentions and actions don't match. The true harm comes not from leaving the task undone, but rather in sustaining our lies to ourselves, in our self-serving justifications.

There will always be good reasons why you didn't do what you said—and they are all distortions of the true reason (that you really didn't want to do whatever it was very much). It doesn't matter whether the deed itself is noble or trivial. The harm comes from how *YOU* feel about not doing it. So DO IT—so you can feel good about yourself again. It takes less energy to do the neglected deed than to handle all the inner turmoil that is created by avoiding it. You'll feel like you've taken off ten-pound boots and be amazed by the amount of energy that is freed for other activities.

Track down those long-avoided tasks and get them done! You'll like yourself a lot better, and feel energized to boot.

Chapter 4

Caramels
Dare to Care

No one lives alone. Many of our challenges or difficulties come from other people. They also can bring us our greatest joys. T'aint easy to develop relationships that "work." Even if we don't try, we still have relationships, they are just the "don't work" kind. We'd like to care—honest. But sometimes the demands they place on us don't seem quite worth it.

Each of us feels a constant tug-of-war between being true to ourselves and our own needs and being accommodating to others. In order to establish strong relationships, we must find ways to achieve both goals at the same time. They needn't be in conflict, but the cost is mutual respect and constant re-adjustments. It's a good thing the payoffs are worth all that effort.

Share your BonBons; they can nurture you just as you nurture those you care about.

In Trust We Trust

Trust is a delicate bond that ties people together. Trust is reciprocal, between equals. Each person has invested something of who they are in the relationship, in the other(s), in the circumstances they have shared. Trust requires each of them to trust and to strive to be trustworthy. Unfortunately, we tend to forget how important it is to be worthy of trust. Trust is not a right, it is achieved and sustained through sincere and caring endeavors.

Trust is active, requiring frequent fresh efforts, watered with honesty and mutual respect. At the point that such efforts cease (by either or both), trust withers, sometimes past reviving. The presence of trust at the start of the relationship does not indicate that it continues. Trust rooted primarily in recollection may be showing that you can no longer trust, or that you trust in the passed tense (past tense). Trust thrives only in the present. It happens now, or not at all.

Trust and trusting are not the same thing. Trusting is passive. It also is not rooted in equality. Whenever you are trusting you are dependent on the other's performance. You have lost some of your power and are vulnerable. When trust has been broken, it must be rebuilt or it will surely die. Being *trusting* is never a satisfactory substitute. Small distinction? Maybe, but one is grounded in strength, and the other invites despair. One is whole, the other is fragmented. It is a distinction worth exploring and maintaining.

When Sharing Isn't Caring

We share to show we care. But not everything shared is good for us—or the relationship. When does sharing make a problem larger or worse?

When you lie, to yourself or to them

When you focus only on negatives

When you complain that there are absolutely no choices available (never true)

When you are critical of yourself or others and only want to get confirmation

When you wallow in self-pity, or regrets, or hope for revenge

When you attempt to place blame on someone or take the blame yourself (ditto for guilt)

When you ponder why something happened instead of figuring out what can be done about it or how to apply your new awareness

When you don't respect the other person or their input and reactions.

When any of these activities occurs among friends, they are a poor use of friendship. Friends are precious, as is the time you share. Bring the best you can to each encounter. Demonstrate you care about what you share. Then you'll both grow stronger—apart as well as together.

Your Impact

Wherever you are, whatever you do, you leave an impact.

Choose it—Leave the impression that *you* want.

Prepare for it—Decide to be the person who CREATES that impression; notice how you're doing it and why you're doing it.

Be alert for it—Treat every experience as a potential adventure.

Find the fun of it—It's available for you and those you touch.

You are known less because of your ideas than by the personal impact you make on those around you. The force of that impact demonstrates your values, your priorities and your personality more clearly than anything you could say.

You don't get to decide the value of your impact; that is determined by those who are affected by it. The person you influence defines what your impact was *for him*, even if it was very different from what was intended. Whenever the two impressions don't match, it is not the receiver's fault. You simply have not yet found the most effective way to express your intention. Figuring out your unique way to express that intent provides the adventure.

If you try to avoid leaving an impression, you will be too passive, unable to react appropriately. You can no longer behave as freely as the situation would permit. A failure to seek opportunities where you leave your impact votes for inertia, for more-of-the-same automatic responses.

Choose to consciously define your impact. Express your unique way of seeing and doing things. If you duck those opportunities, if you fail to assert WHO you are, you could become superfluous, even in your own life.

So develop a flair! Make a statement as unique as you are. Create a noteworthy presence—just by being you, *intentionally.*

Watered Silk

The following poem was written by my daughter, Jessica, some years ago to commemorate a special occasion. I share it, along with the hope that it will enliven the memories you have lovingly stored away.

Watered Silk

A wedding, a delicate tooth, a precious story.

We collect these tangibles and hold them gingerly
between our fingers.

Then we hide them away—

a tooth wrapped in a handkerchief in the bottom of
a vase,

reminders hidden not because they are shameful secrets

but because they are *too* precious.

We collect so many things—

tarnished, graying objects, fraying silks

and even the gentle expressions you offered to us
yesterday.

Please, let us take these precious, calming memories
out of the boxes,

out of the hidden places and cherish them—

press them hard against our palms, against our cheeks

and exclaim loyalty for these objects that have become
family.

This old porcelain tooth, smooth from a child's open
    mouth and left behind.
These silks, yellowing scrapbooks and silver ladles to
    share warming soups fill up our houses.
They will always remain there, like little voices trapped
below the inverted glasses in the cupboards.

Take them out before the guests arrive.

Let us wrap ourselves in the watered silk,
    once saved for a sacred dress
and then tell stories about a child who left behind a
    treasured tooth.

Those memories do not slip or fade.
They bloom like a wedding, like a parcel waiting to be
    opened—
a warm flower, a bunch of yellow daffodils, ready to open
    new memories
    and protect those left behind.

Jessica J. Grant
June 1992

No Lip Service

Whenever someone speaks to you:

Ask yourself what REALLY is being said.

Don't just listen to the words, the content.

Listen to the emotion behind the words.

Listen also to the unstated concerns—what they are avoiding saying.

Listen to what they say is needed, while knowing that is not all they desire.

Before you respond, ask yourself, "What do they want from me?"

Respect

To be heard with an open mind

To be treated as though they have a point and I can "get it"

To have their concern taken seriously—it IS important just as THEY are important

Only then should you respond. Because now you respond directly to THEM, not just their words.

The Ties That Bind

Each of us needs to feel connected—to our family, community, ethnic, social and work contacts. Our sense of belonging gives us a safety net and context from which we can gain invisible, as well as visible, support. Even when we dislike some of those bonds and feel them as restraints, they still diminish our fundamental sense of isolation.

The tragedy of the homeless wanderers or of the disintegrating city dwellers or of any unloved person is that most of the connections of these individuals have been ruptured. Mobility erodes the family closeness; broken homes undermine a loving family support system; "me-first" philosophies lead to decisions that disregard the consequences of choices on others affected by them. Such decisions end up destroying both trust and a sense of responsibility.

We have been short-changed. In the elusive quest to be free we too casually sacrifice our connectedness, and thereby a bit of our humanity. No amount of money can heal those wounds. Only new emotional and caring connections can start the healing process. Every living person is capable of reconnecting himself with his larger context. Each of us has a daily responsibility to do so.

Reach out. Reknit broken links. Build new connections. As you weave, you will receive.

What Does a Kind Word Cost?

What perverse aspect of our character makes us want to thwart those close to us—to withhold the thing they hunger for? What makes us withhold something which we have in our power to give freely? Each of us, in many verbal and nonverbal ways, communicates to those around us what we really want. Usually it is simple: notice me, appreciate me, respect me; tell me I'm pretty, or strong, or liked.

The message is sent out, riding on each comment, gesture, request. We do not need to know a person well to recognize that hitchhiking message—it screams at us. It says: "This is what I need from you." And then, what do we give them? ANYTHING BUT THAT! Why is that? Do we get power from withholding?

When I was a teenager, whenever a reward or recognition came to me, my mother would say "You couldn't have done it without me, could you." Obviously, the answer was, "Of course, I couldn't have done it without you." I never gave her the satisfaction of that response.

It took many years and a good dose of maturity to see that giving my mother that satisfaction in no way diminished me. Several years ago I tried an idea that enriched both our lives. I resolved that in every conversation with her, I would find a sincere way to say the words, "I couldn't have done _____ (whatever it was, and it didn't matter how minor it was) without you." Before long something very intangible but longstanding between us relaxed, and we found a more solid basis for our relationship.

It didn't take long for me to see that withholding appropriate responses to another hurt me more than it hurt them. A kind response to another's need is easy to do and requires so little—only a willingness to respond to another's need.

One Versus Many

I touch a lot of people every day, but I never touch a group. No organization can ever be more important than EACH ONE of its members. The group should devote the combined efforts toward supporting *their* needs and concerns. The pooled power that emerges through their shared goals and visions is capable of improving the lives and opportunities of *every one* of the members. Belonging permits each to share with other like-minded members. NEVER should the group place any other priorities higher than those. Especially, it must never sacrifice individual members to other goals.

Look at the organizations you've joined. Are they serving you and your priorities, or are you just serving theirs? You deserve the support and cooperation of like-minded members. Don't let yourself be manipulated. Make sure you receive a valuable return for the time and effort invested in any organization.

Charity

Charity *cannot* be impersonal. It emerges through the kindness one human being shares with another. It is transmitted through the sense of concern we offer. Charity need not involve money. If it does, the money should be secondary to the giver's recognition of the receiver as a person.

We give best when offering something of ourselves. That is why impersonal institutions or government agencies are so incapable of performing effectively in this arena. Caring and sharing reflect the emotional responses we make to the experiences of life. Charity is not an isolated and separate activity. Rather, it acknowledges our awareness of our own connections with the world, our roots and other people. The more strongly we feel those connections, the more we seek opportunities to be kind—and to share.

Whenever you sense an urge to give, give of yourself. Give your time, your energy, your sincere emotional support, as well as money or things. Such charity rewards you both. Such personal contact connects you and also reconnects your humanity.

Give and Take

The world is full of GIVERS and TAKERS. One problem with our country today is the tendency for some people to act as though democracy gives them the right to be takers. The emphasis on having "rights" further strengthens the taker mentality.

Each of us comes into life as a taker because a child can do little else. But we're designed to grow mature enough and generous enough and caring enough and capable enough to eventually become givers. You cannot become a giver until you stop being a taker. What you receive in return is the ability to experience life beyond your own self-centered needs.

The bigger picture, which includes the influences of others about you, starts to matter: your family, your community, your friends, your religious and ethnic ties. You see yourself involved in a meaningful context, where WHAT you are and WHO you are have significant value. You recognize that you have much that is unique and precious to give and to share. Such a broadening of awareness signals the real shift to personal and social maturity. Democracy depends on citizens with that scope of vision. But it is not possible when the government, the family or other social institutions nurture the taking philosophy.

Look around and seek out the infinite little ways you can give—a kind word, a nod of encouragement, an acknowledgment of progress, a listening ear. They don't take much time or energy but pay huge rewards, every time you make the effort to be a giver.

Hate Happens
When Love Doesn't

Hate is what happens when the opportunities to behave in a loving and caring way are not noticed or exercised. The range of love from kindness through passion can only exist when ACTIVELY performed— they don't arise passively. The disintegration of positive ideals, which are unable to take root through behavior, leaves a void. The failure of love and kindness to AGGRESSIVELY override and replace habitual resentments creates a vacuum, which calls forth the forces of hate in all their petty forms.

We may not be motivated to hate, but it arises like an insidious weed if we fail to cultivate a crop of goodwill. Only positive and sustained efforts can uproot the tendrils of hate, lurking, awaiting our lapse of vigilance to spread and grow.

Seven Flavors of Icky

From time to time, I find myself unable to do anything that works. It is a shock for a capable person like my usual self to feel so totally ineffective. I have learned to recognize it as final exam time, yet I am not the primary one being tested.

I see myself firmly impaled like a worm on a hook—alive but helpless. Then I'm tossed in among my daily associates. How they treat me is the real point of the test. What they do to me while I'm in that impotent state is the true measure of THEIR (not my) level of growth.

I may be "stuck," but that doesn't make me deaf, blind or stupid. Perhaps my restriction makes me more perceptive, for I see clearly (and hence the world can also see) their "true" reactions. Strangely, almost everyone treats me as though I can't tell the difference.

There are several types of treatment.

1. Those who kick while they can—small people who take advantage of the temporary situation for their own benefit.

2. Those who, accustomed to being given energy or help, are willing to continue taking, even to my last drop.

3. Those so out of touch they are unaware that anything is different.

4. Those who give lip service of solace or assistance, but whose words don't match their behavior.

5. Those who offer the kind cliches, but who then undercut me emotionally and as a person.

6. Those who give grudging assistance and then assertively distance themselves, fearing more may be needed.

7. Those who attempt to say and do the "right" thing, but in the process of insincere "helping" destroy what little dignity that remains.

8. Those who see me as the same person as ever, but now, because I can only receive, willingly support me in any way they can. These people are few but very special, and worth the pain of the experience.

The test for me is to endure without judging, to permit the testing without feeling I'm being punished (I'm not) or that I am wrong (I'm not). Whenever I see someone "on the hook," I sincerely try to treat that person with love and support. That's the only way to demonstrate that I understand the test and know the answer.

Enjoy the View

Visualize a large mansion with many windows facing out in all directions. Anyone inside is free to look out any window in any direction and to select the view they prefer. Each of us has our familiar window that we have chosen to look through most of the time. Usually, we assume our window is the same one used by those around us, and that we're all looking out at the same view. It comes as a jolting surprise, like a double-take, whenever we discover that other people can't see what is so obvious and "there" to us.

Only at such times are we reminded how much of what we see is determined by where we're seeing it from, that is, our own assumptions and values. We glimpse those personal influences momentarily and quickly resume our assumption that our view is the "real" one, accurately showing what is out there. The benefit of walking a mile in someone else's moccasins is not so much to see from their window (perspective) as to be able to rediscover our own unstated perspective when we return to it.

Sometimes we have a favorite window that makes us feel special and tranquil—we save it for special occasions. We remember fondly what it felt like to be there and how the world looks from there. Why don't we go there more often, instead of saving it for special times?

Sometimes, with a close friend, we leave our familiar window and find one we both look out of together. The view is made even richer by the ability to share it, by the opportunity to express our reactions and exchange with another who "sees what we do."

Ah . . . , the delight enhances the view!

Chapter 5

Mints

Embracing Life's Best Mo-Mints

Change is an unavoidable fact of life, but growth is optional. Once we reach adulthood, physical growth is minimal. But the opportunities for mental, emotional and spiritual growth do not cease. We discover them as we embrace life fully. Such inner enjoyment and growth continue as long as we make any efforts to pursue them. They connect us with the rewards we seek. Life's best mo-mints are constantly offered, but we have to s t r e t c h for them. There is no danger of running out, since they can be found in any situation, any social interaction, any awareness. Like a mint, they will add spice and sparkle to your life.

Uncommonly Common?

Common sense is a most misunderstood idea. It is extraordinarily rare (not common at all), since it is grounded in undistorted truth. It is simple, direct and lacks pretense. It occurs only when there is clear and direct vision coupled with an absence of preconceptions. In fact, common sense is a form of wisdom, and just as hard to come by.

Most of what passes as common sense is rooted in adages, which are reflexively trotted out at appropriate occasions, without reflection or fresh awareness. It rests on old, familiar, stale information and clichés rather than fresh, focused awareness. Oh yes, the counterfeit common sense is common enough, but it usually lacks sense.

Every time you engage yourself in understanding yourself, those around you, life, nature or timeless ideas, you connect with your own common sense. Then you are not fooled by the counterfeit forms that come along.

A Test-A-Minute

Life is a series of tests. Your day is a series of tests. Knowing there is a test in progress creates new options for you—most of which have nothing to do with pass or fail (which is seldom the point of any meaningful test). For example:

Am I making good use of my opportunities?

Is time my "enemy" or "friend"?

Am I creating problems for those around me—do they have to "pick up" or adjust when I pass by?

Am I having fun or creating a happy space?

Am I wiser than the last time this happened?

Can I improve on what's happening here? Then, what's stopping me?

Am I aware—tuned to both the big picture and little nuances of what's going on?

Am I bothering to be nice or helpful or supportive?

Is this worth doing or is there something else more
important for me to do?

You get to take any test you want as often as you
want. You even get to score it on any basis you want.
As you grade your tests, you become less inclined to
judge yourself and more inclined to understand your-
self. There are no wrong answers, but some sure feel
RIGHT!

Ode to Being "Had"

TOO GOOD TO BE TRUE! What do those words mean to you? Not true? Unable to be trusted? Counterfeit? Naive? Con game?

Most people will lose interest in something that appears to be "too good to be true." It doesn't make sense; in fact, it offends your good sense. You'd be a fool to trust it, downright gullible. Besides, down deep you feel you ought to know better.

"Too good to be true" is a tug-of-war between hope and logic. It is the conflict between what you would like to happen (indeed a fragile, often forlorn hope) and all the reasons it won't or couldn't happen. Logic can be 100% true, yet in such cases I prefer to discount it. Reason can only deal in probabilities, not certainties.

There is a slender window of opportunity where logic can be skirted. A crack of possibilities through the impenetrable (impossible) exists and can be found. As long as you place your trust in hope, desire or determination it is not closed to you. To accept the voice of logic means the attempt isn't even made.

I know the value of intellect, but it is not wise and cannot comprehend vain hope or the human drama from which it arises. It will disregard the improbable in favor of the likely. If I am to err, it will always be for the dream, the wish, the hope, the long shot. When nurtured and acted on with determination, such notions can have greater power than the forces that impede

them. Logic does not and cannot understand this—
but I do.

Too good to be true? Yes, but that need not mean
unattainable. It IS possible, though reaching that goal
is far from reliable or effortless. Sometimes you get to
discover that what you pursued with such single-minded
determination is both good (actually wonderful) and
true. That is the victory of personal vision over reason.
That is the rare and elusive reward for persisting in
your folly.

BEWARE: Watch out for con men; they love people
like us. Caution is advised.

Hark . . . Who Speaks There?

A while back, when my daughter, Jessica, was a teenager she applied for a job. The owner of the business was outspokenly bigoted and disparaging to women. Jessica was torn between wanting the job and fearing the daily indignities she could expect if hired. She asked me: "Should I take the job?" Here's what I told her.

You have to decide for yourself, and it's up to you to understand *why* you made that choice. You can take the job for the right reasons or for the wrong reasons. You can decide *not* to take the job for the right reasons or for the wrong reasons. WHAT you decide is less important than knowing the REASONS for your decision.

Some voice within you (some part of yourself) will become stronger and you will start trusting it more. Other voices within you (parts of yourself) will become weaker and less able to influence your decisions. The choice of which voices you decide to listen to within yourself will build your character and influence each choice to come. Start noticing what parts of yourself become stronger each time a choice is made. That awareness will make you potent.

By the way, she didn't take the job, but the process she went through continues to influence her daily.

Civilization

The measure of each civilization is whether it provides reasons for each person to make the efforts to rise beyond the easy, the passive, the familiar and convenient answers. Will it encourage progress or regression? Hard-wired into each of us are two contradictory impulses. One pulls toward childish self-centered pleasures and quick, easy answers. The other impulse is toward growth, with an eye focused on the long-term benefits for everyone. They both have rewards and trade-offs, consequences and costs.

How do you think our civilization is doing? Is that O.K. with you?

Gravity Is Heavy

Gravity is the natural force which pulls us down and holds us there. It is interesting that the same word is used for the downward pull of mental seriousness. A weighty matter, if taken seriously, will force us down, down, down. Hello, gloom and doom. The mental and physical pulls of inertia are unremitting, undeniable, and in the end inevitable, that is unless. . .

UNLESS we assert the effort to *want* something else (almost anything else) and want it so badly that we will challenge ourselves to override that downward pull and our own reluctance to act.

UNLESS we are willing to learn from children, the only things that gravity cannot grab, who constantly look up, see with awe, demonstrate the upward force of growth, and show that life can be fun. It is children who can raise us, if we can abandon the notion that we raise them.

UNLESS we can seek, find and remember every day that our willing efforts make a difference, though short-lived, against the weight of entropy (the tendency of energy to run down and stop) and discouragement.

UNLESS we learn that the omnipresent enemy is a passive, mindless force that can be briefly defeated by ANY ACTIVE EFFORT we choose to make. We have to repeatedly assert ourselves and our values. We have to fight the external and internal urges to relax our vigilance against indifference.

If we can't muster the will to sustain the unremitting effort to go UP or STAY UP, well, then D

O

W

N we go.

Getting All You Pay For

Some of life's most valuable and precious lessons can only be learned by failure. If we then sink too deeply into disappointment or embrace self-pity, we fail to get the message that we have paid such a high price to receive. Insist not just that the suffering stop, but that a lesson is received for each setback. Most people are satisfied just to have the difficulty go away, even at the risk that it will return.

Unless we insist that we learn the meaningful message that comes through suffering, we haven't gotten the benefit we "paid" so dearly for. It is not possible to prevent some of life's upsets, but we can demand that we get an understanding from them. Hold on until you can say, with sincerity (you have to really mean it): "Painful as it was, I'm glad it happened, or I wouldn't have learned *_____." Whatever you say to fill in the blank is a trophy you can use forever—you've earned it, and it is valuable beyond price. That is the way that wisdom is achieved.

We have the right to hold the universe accountable for the lessons it sends us, and it will give us a valuable answer—but only when we insist.

*It's for you to decide; fill in your own blank.

I Speak; Therefore I Become

We do violence to any experience when we reduce it to words. The fullness of the experience and all its complexity becomes less complete as we attempt to express it. Yet, the effort to express it adds to and alters the initial experience—leading to a new personalized version that is, in certain ways, even more complete. Our experience changes us, and the struggle to express what we have experienced further alters both us and that initial experience. Such expression furthers the growth of understanding and awareness. Such is the way we ACTIVELY create our lives.

Take the time to relive valued experiences and give words to them. Fix them in memory, anchored by your words. Don't stop there—tell someone else and see how their reaction further enlarges the event. As you continue to speak of them you enliven and recreate the events of your life. Truly, your experiences continue to grow and become more powerful. You can say, "I speak; therefore I become."

Me as an Amoeba

Don't abdicate involvement in what happens to you. Of course, you have to have the good sense to move away from things that hurt you. Even an amoeba (one-celled animal) will move away from irritations. But, you can't live life like an amoeba, simply avoiding unpleasantness. That strategy permits every undesirable situation to dictate your behavior for you. It permits you to exercise neither your will nor your judgment.

How much better to be attracted to the things you like (positive) instead of simply and constantly avoiding the unpleasant (negative). However, to shift attention to the positive (the goalpost) you have to WANT something even more than you dislike life's irritations. You must WANT something even more than your comfort, and then focus all of your attention and energy on achieving it. You put it first, despite the discomforts that accompany your efforts. You find ways to remind yourself of your determination and reinforce it, over and over and over again.

Otherwise, old habits and reactions will reflexively eliminate all your other choices. Even a choice which proves disappointing serves you better than a mindless habit. The mindless behavior will re-assert itself at every moment you are not vigilant, ready to assert an intelligent, determined preference. Sure, getting what you want is frustrating, often elusive, but it sure beats living like an amoeba.

Phony Choices

You have just found yourself in a very unpleasant situation, painted into a corner, without any palatable choices. You've made your best efforts to work it out— and failed. It feels awful; you feel defeated, lonely, scared, but even worse, you feel foolish. "How can a halfway intelligent person make such a mess of things?"

From time to time each of us has found ourselves in such a fix. The significant issue is not how you got into the soup, but rather what you choose to do next. Are you focusing on the failure or on the unanticipated opportunity that is always lurking in its shadow?

There is a temptation at such times to look back and puzzle over how we got there, to examine the choices we "should have made." We are inclined to conclude, in retrospect, that we're wrong to be in this fix because there are right choices we "should have made." Beware! That is a trap of the rational (and rationalizing) mind.

Despite what we like to think, few of our decisions are ever made for logical or rational reasons. More often, we decide on the basis of emotion, self-image or other people's expectations. Later, if things don't turn out well, we so badly want to make sense of our pain that we look for something or someone to blame, often ourselves. We want to be able to say: "If I had made another choice this wouldn't have happened." Nonsense!

Each of us *always* makes the best choice considering WHO WE ARE and the facts as they exist for us AT THE TIME. (It is also true that there are always more available choices than there appear to be. There are NEVER only two choices, even though that's the way it often seems.) But when we look back, we are inclined to wonder, for example: "Why did I marry Pete instead of _____ (going to college, marrying Steve, becoming a nurse, etc.)" or "Why didn't I choose a career that pays more money?" We mis-remember. Given the choices we *actually got* we *always* picked the one we thought would be the better one. There were reasons we didn't select the other alternatives, but those reasons are seldom filed in memory.

Choices are easy in hindsight. But choices are actually made without hindsight, based on the information as we know it AT THE TIME.

Another mental trickery says, "I could have chosen differently, and then I would be _____ [rich or happily married, or respected etc. (a totally fictional alternative outcome)]." The truth is, that option wasn't offered as one of the perceived choices. No ninny will say, "I'll marry George so I can have a miserable life instead of being rich and successful." The choices we make are those we think will bring us what we want. Whenever you compare real with fiction, the fictional possibility looks like the "right" choice. But you never actually had that choice, so stop regretting that you failed to take it.

Anyone can learn to make better choices, but not in the past. We must make them as they come along. Our sincerity, character and attention to details improve our ability to choose. And these are skills that grow as we do—not in retrospect.

Let's Disagree

I love it when someone does not agree with me. They are about to show me another point of view— one that has new elements, new emphasis, new conclusions. I am more interested in strengthening my understanding than in proving I am right or they are wrong.

When I am not defensive about the opinions I hold, then disagreement is not a threat. After all, "I am not my opinions." As I grow and change, so will they. The key is to respect the other person and their different point of view—not to judge them, not to reject them. I need to make mental space for them. When we have a sincere dialogue I find myself s t r e t c h i n g mentally. I am eager to see what I haven't yet seen or find an unfamiliar way to view what I've already seen. There is no danger that I'll forget my opinion while I lay it aside. What's more likely is that I'll develop a fuller, more complete opinion than I started with.

Here's how to tell whether you're having a dialogue or an argument. In an argument you hear a lot of "but . . . but . . . but . . .," which negates the other person's arguments. Each "but" acts as a brake. With dialogue you hear "and . . . and . . . and . . ." Each "and" acts as an accelerator, increasing your interest. By using "and" the speaker recognizes the other person's points and embellishes them. Whenever you are both embellishing a point, you create together something that is new, beautiful and unexpected. You also discover other areas of agreement you wouldn't otherwise have noticed. You both transcend the initial point of discussion and discover a larger shared view.

So, look for opportunities to disagree—as long as you mind your "buts" and give rein to your "ands." You'll rediscover why communication is such a treat and worth any amount of effort.

Lurking, Lurking, Lurking

Lurking, lurking, lurking in the murky murky depths, below the surface, just out of sight is a gnawing, groaning sense of unease. In the dark of the night, when all else is quiet, you barely hear them moaning: "Ooooh . . . Ooooh . . ." "What about the bills?" "Ooooh . . . Ooooh . . ." "There's nothing you can do about your boss, kids, future, etc." "Ooooh . . . Ooooh . . ." Such gnawing refrains flit through your mind, constricting your heart, paralyzing your confidence. You're being visited by your own subterranean monsters. "Ooooh . . ."

They are real, sort of, at home in your deep dark recesses, out of your sight, but not out of your mind. But they cannot survive in the light. Shine some light, some focused attention in there and they are seen to be as concrete as shadows. Their power depends on them staying unclear, *barely* articulated.

Don't avoid them; that's what keeps them functioning, instilling fear. Confront them. Demand they speak up— state their case, make the fears explicit. Put the spotlight on what they say. They probably are not valid concerns (if they are, by all means deal with them). More likely, they are only immature, not-quite-rational notions. Say, "Thank you, I hear what you say and will consider your input. Let me handle it, I know what to do."

Once you've heard them, you've been liberated. They lose their power over you. There is nothing further they can do to you. If they come back, say it again, as often as necessary. You REALLY are more potent than your fears, once you see them in the light.

Haven't Got the Tim*ing*

We will give up our time much more willingly than we will ever give up our TIMING. We carefully dole out our time like money, spending some on this or that, more here, none there; but we consciously spend it. We know we're making trade-offs, trying to satisfy the competing demands on our time, our energy, our lives, hoping there will be enough to go around. It's full of tough choices, but we understand about spending time, carefully portioning out our hours and minutes.

In each thing we do we express our timing. The rate at which I do a thing is "the way I do it." We don't question our timing because it is invisible to us. It has become part of who we are and whatever we do. We have gradually consigned most of our timing options to the blind operation of habit. In the process, we have lost our power to alter our speed except under extraordinary situations (such as great danger).

Yet, if we can change our timing, we can increase our ability to alter the way events impact us. Whether we speed up or slow down, whether we make a large or small change, we have altered our customary reaction pattern. In so doing, we have gotten our finger back on the controls. Now we can choose the rate at which we respond and thereby have reasserted a degree of control in life usually denied us. We can DECIDE to match or alter the speed at which our choices are made and then consciously choose how to proceed. In that small measure of freedom, we find we can make freer, more relevant choices.

Our timing is a small matter, but we are governed by it. Try taking back control of it and you'll really see who is in charge. It is hard work to wrest a fragment of change in timing, and no victory lasts. But watch your timing; it's your direct path to freedom.

Chapter 6

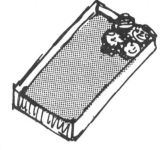

Assorted
Miscellaneous Flavors

The contents of this chapter is the most like life—
an array of various impressions without structured order.
You bring the structure to events by the way you perceive,
react and then remember them. Your style of interac-
tion with life changes both you and your surroundings.
A single event can yield an infinite variety of responses,
but by choosing particular ones, you simultaneously
create and are created by your world.

BonBons can be found wherever you experience
an event fully. But it is a special delight to discover
them in familiar places, where you never noticed them
before. Treat your life like an Easter egg hunt, where
you happen upon the special tidbits, the BonBons
awaiting you.

These assorted BonBons are one-of-a-kind. Each
flavor is as unique as you are, as unique as each day
is, as unique as every moment is. Variety encourages
surprises. With variety you are most likely to find the
unexpected.

Busy, Busy, Busy

We get swept up in the demands of our constantly-busy lives, that leak into each minute and demand we respond. Not enough time, not enough energy, not enough attention—so we feel pushed, pulled, driven and pressured. Nothing we could do would be sufficient.

Say, ENOUGH!

You cannot do it all. So do as much as you can, knowing you can get more out of whatever you're already doing. You can silence the voices that drive you—for a moment.

Find a few seconds of breathing space in each little activity. Hold yourself apart long enough to pause and remember yourself. You neutralize the mounting frenzy each busy moment that you pause to enjoy or reflect. It needn't take long. Reclaim the crumbs of time that feed your heart, that reconnect you with timeless eternity. You'll still be busy and your days will be full. But you'll also experience reminders of what's really important, after all.

What You Need to Know About a Bad Day

They come for no apparent reason, and can leave for the same reason.

There is nothing wrong with you because they come.

Fault and blame have nothing to do with it.

It's optional—it's not a bad day unless or until YOU SAY SO, so avoid saying so.

If you can't change the day, change your outlook. Change where you have placed your attention.

This is the time for a good laugh. Find the humor in what is happening to you. Make someone laugh and laugh along. If you can, laugh at yourself. Laugh long and often.

It's not the end of the world. It's temporary, and probably not nearly as bad as it looks.

Don't condemn an entire day because of a few unpleasant little events.

Don't add up all the unpleasantness. That may be all you see at the moment, but not all that is there. Instead, notice the interspersed good things.

Keep busy; it's hard to feel bad when you don't have time for it. Self-pity or discouragement are luxuries few people can afford.

Do something for someone worse off than you are, and you'll get some perspective.

Take the time to notice all the things you have to be grateful for. Bask in the things that are healthy and working in your life.

Designated Driver

Each of us is either NEED driven or VISION driven. The difference between them appears small, but like a fork in the road, will lead to radically different life views and dramatically different outcomes. Whatever drives you influences your every choice and determines where you eventually arrive.

If you have ever been fired by a personal vision or a burning desire, you treat it as more important than anything else in your life. Its primacy makes all other choices secondary to it. Each event is interpreted as whether it will further the accomplishment of that goal. Even trivial choices thereby become charged with direction and relevance. Often, the achievement of the vision or desire is less important than the way it animates and makes purposeful all the other parts of your life. You feel a positive pull toward the distant, but discernible, realm where your vision can flower.

Your vision need not be about major long-term life goals. It may be expressed in as simple a manner as the way you live and function. For example, if you choose to be careful and attentive to the emotional needs of those around you, it will influence all your social interactions. Any heartfelt resolve can be the way you express and demonstrate that personal vision.

Lacking a vision leaves you to be need driven. Steady physical and psychological demands can control you, for they are not subordinated to an overriding purpose. When the hungers and fears arise, you feel compelled to satisfy them to reduce their discomfort. That is, you act to cancel the negative urges, to avoid the unpleasant rather than to achieve a desired benefit. Such needs keep you busy, but provide slight satisfaction, leaving you enslaved and driven.

Which drives you? How much control of your choices does it leave you?

Problem Solving or Problem D'Solving*

Sometimes people who are good at solving problems do not REALLY want their problems gone. They want to have the problem so that they can have the satisfaction of solving it, even more than they want a remedy. Ask yourself: would you rather be able to solve a particular problem or not have had the problem at all?

We get a lot of satisfaction and power from solving a problem. We feel good about ourselves and feel in control as the problem is "solved." Every problem is tailored to fit the individual precisely. It arises as an interaction of a unique person and a customized circumstance.

Each problem is a message stating: "What is happening doesn't work." It demands your attention. If you want it to be gone you have to find out why it's happening to you. Without looking at HOW or WHY it arose, we have done nothing to alter the underlying cause of the problem. It is likely to re-emerge in the same or different forms over and over again.

Problem solving looks at the effects or symptoms and attempts to make changes there. Problem d'solving* works by changing the underlying causes. Problem d'solving focuses beyond the specific problem to the bigger context which helped to cause it. What is at the root? What really is going on here? You start noticing that there are logical explanations, and that the problem is an appropriate reaction to the existing underlying conditions. Only changes made on that deeper, usually invisible, level can eliminate a recurrence of the problem. As in gardening, one approach is like trimming back weeds and the other is like pulling them up by the roots.

Even more important, with problem d'solving* you find there are many approaches and answers available. You have more control and can select those answers offering extra advantages. You can apply as many solutions as you like. You no longer fear a problem because as you attempt to eliminate it, it helps you see more than before. As the Problem D'Solver* says, "You're not done until you're glad you had the problem." You see the initial problem as something you have outgrown, as something that no longer has the power to cause you difficulty.

*trademark of Lynella Grant

Wake-Up Call

Each day when you wake up there is a new world ready for you. Your battery has been recharged, so your mind is clear, the frustrations and bruises of yesterday seem far away. Feel fresh, with a sense of expectancy for what awaits, like a child with boundless energy and enthusiasm, who is unfettered by life's burdens. The challenge of each day is to see how long you can sustain the fresh new start. How far can its initial momentum go?

Keeping the precious innocent, unlimited sense of fresh beginnings is a deliberate choice. Like any other choice, it helps to prefer it, want it, sacrifice for it and decline whatever contradicts it. Demands can't be permitted to sap the precious energy. The pristine perspective (a fragile treasure) can be hoarded. As you enjoy it, it does not dwindle. It enlivens you and whatever you pursue.

Sure, it's mighty hard to keep it. Most days that fresh energy is gone in a twinkle. But, just *wanting* to sustain it, wanting to stay fresh stretches the attention, the alertness. It remains at the level of choice, where you ask: "Do I want this more than anything else?" The repeated attempts to choose it keep it close and energizing.

How long until it is forgotten and it flies away? Probably you won't even notice, not until your energy has dwindled and the day has turned ordinary. Pause to realize you can still choose how you spend the rest of your time and energy. Be glad—in the morning it all is back again. Keep taking those steps forward. There's a fresh start and a fresh outlook offered every day and a potent way to proceed through the inevitable ups and downs.

Yes, there will be ups and downs, ups and downs, ups and downs. But take that first step, confident that your journey will reward you: new experiences, personal growth, challenging companions, intrigue, detours filled with adventures. If you're to reach your destination, you will use everything you've brought, and more. But your journey will ceaselessly reward and renew you.

Smash the Mid-Range

Awareness doesn't work like an off-on switch—it's a continuum. One end is dead or close to it, like sleep. The other end is heightened perception, filled with inexpressible joy. Between them we live—with our awareness fluctuating: notice, distracted, drifting, daydreaming, attentive, vague, focused. We shift; we drift.

Many days awareness comes, flits in and out, turned down like a pilot light ready to ignite when interest summons it. Attention is "On Call," waiting to be roused from its daydreams, so close to the sleep end of the scale. Habit runs the show, leaving little room for innovation or flexibility. We get through the day, sort of, without noticing all that happens to us. Aware, yes—but just barely.

Could that possibly be enough? Awareness is such a powerful tool it can deliver much much more, into our lives, into our days, into every minute. Crank it up— push it to reveal the rich texture available in each event, each person, each idea you encounter. Engage every one of your senses and your mind at the same time. Penetrate beyond superficial impressions. See, hear, feel, sense, notice what else is present also— sensations more subtle, yet very real. Pause to register and enjoy. Experience intently and intensely, basking in whatever you discover. All that you feel now can be even more enhanced. As awareness is sharpened, held and focused on the details, it shifts. Then a bigger, more complete and complex picture forms. You can get better at it simply by practicing it and enjoying it. Your capacity to live fully is much greater than routinely used.

Mostly, we stay in the middle of the scale—aware, alert, but filtering out details we don't think we need. But the wonder and the fullness are not there. They are up the scale of awareness, where we become fully involved. Why not live there, since it takes no longer, but provides so much more?

Life Is But a Stream

Everyone starts life as a curious, creative, endlessly exploring bundle of energy. Gradually we are tamed—civilized to live in a home, a family, a risky world. Somewhere along the way the taming shuts down our abilities to explore and create spontaneously. Such impulses become dammed up behind the structures we create and that are imposed upon us, for our own good, of course.

Like a free-running stream that is channeled and then piped, the water may still trickle out at the end—but it's not the same stream. It is still water, but what has become of the meadow, the birdsong, the rippling surface, the minnows, the bundle of energy that made the stream vibrant and sparkling? These count for nothing if you only measure the stream as gallons of water.

That dammed-up stream is like the gifted child that resides below the surface of our daily lives. Beauty, fun, a world of wonder are sacrificed within the "shoulds" and "should nots" that dictate our lives. Yes, it may be the same stream, but in every way that relates to beauty, or fun, or a world of wonder for the little live and growing things, there is no comparison.

As adults we rarely question our confinements. We move freely it seems; but in reality it is from tank (home) to cistern (work), to holding tanks (our various activities) by pipelines (routes, decisions) established long ago.

Yes, it is still life, our life—if measured by quantity. But what has become of the rest? Take time every day to let loose the curious, creative, endlessly exploring child within. Read a book. Solve a mystery. Be creative: quilt, sew, build an engine, fly a kite or just meander down a path or sit by a stream.

Take Your Vitamins?

The way a person relates to God is a lot like the way they relate to taking vitamins. You get to decide whether you need to take them or not. Or you can ignore the whole issue. You may feel that eating nutritious meals is enough to make you healthy. You may feel that you need additional vitamins every day. Or you may take them at special times, like when you've been sick or run down.

Some people have no idea about whether they need them, so they take them "just to be on the safe side," like buying insurance coverage. Others swear they can feel the energizing benefits and promise they'll do the same for you. Don't count on the experts to guide you, since they can't agree. The research studies contradict each other.

In much the same way as vitamins, you get to decide whether to relate to God: ignore the issue, consider it important or not, a daily need or an occasional boost. Is there an advantage gained from taking large doses? How could you prove it, either way? Maybe it's like a placebo that helps only because you think it will.

Wherever you stand, it is entirely your choice—and only you can tell whether you notice a benefit.

Trust the Warmth— Whatever Its Name

I cannot understand those who are avowed atheists. Is it possible that God in some form has not touched their lives? What accounts for their assurance that God is absent—for everyone? How can they be so sure? It makes as much sense as starting a club to espouse, "There is no daylight—no sun," denying the existence of God.

Some people may join and be fully persuaded. Even if they can't see it, do they also fail to feel its warmth, unable to see the plants it makes grow or to notice the impact in other peoples' lives? Can all such experiences be dismissed as mere superstition?

Am I less intelligent than they who deny they see the sun? We may inhabit the same world but live in vastly different perceptions of it. It matters not what the sun is called. To refuse to feel its heat leaves us cold and alone.

Everything You Need to Know About Customer Service

Drive down any street; on both sides are businesses competing for your dollars. They have their beckoning signs, their displayed inventories, their trained employees, their promotional strategies all focused on luring the customer and making the sale. If they fail to capture sufficient customer interest and enough dollars, the business dies.

Whenever customers or clients come, they have one overriding unstated concern: MAKE ME GLAD I CAME HERE. Every employee in that business should strive to figure out how to accomplish that. It is their primary job function, no matter what the job description says.

In a restaurant, for instance, the food should be at least adequate in taste and appearance; the mood should be comfortable, clean and inviting; the service should be prompt, efficient and performed with thoughtful concern. The ideal is achieved when every part of the dining experience matches (or exceeds) the customer's expectations. When it works, the person with the money is glad to be paying for what he gets. If there are any surprises, they had better be good ones.

If you want to stay in business the corollary rule is: WHATEVER YOU DO, DON'T MAKE ME SORRY I CAME HERE. You don't just lose a customer, you make an enemy—and they can do your business untold damage.

Anyone who runs any kind of business, or provides any kind of service, or works for someone who does, (even the government) ignores this advice at their peril.

Higher Education

We've failed all the children regarding their higher education. Even the good students who get to go to college or get good grades seldom learn about the higher, nobler and more personally enhancing aspects of their natures. Build up their indomitable spirits, enriched emotions, awareness of community and ennobling values. Help them to discover their own abilities to act as positive forces.

That is what education is for. Train them. Fill them with knowledge, certainly. But build the person and show him his worth. That's the kind of education that develops a person aware of his higher nature. That student has received a higher education.

Politics Riddle

Politics is the almost-exclusive preserve of those men who seek to exploit the power of an organization or government for personal gain. Consider what would be possible if that available power were directed to unselfish goals, where significant concerns could be pursued for broad public benefit, where solutions of the "tough problems" were the actual goals. Imagine if expediency and short-sighted fixes were relinquished for value-based and human-enhancing answers.

Would that still be politics?

Control

Life swirls and lurches. Often all we can do is hang on, get along and do the best we can. Not for a minute do we feel we "hold the reins" (reigns). It's enough to hang on to the saddle—to avoid being thrown off. The pace is numbing, the intensity befuddling, the choices unrelenting.

Do I exaggerate? Is it even true sometimes? What can keep life from running away with us?

Such a pace creates a "bail-the-boat," "deal-with-the-crises" mentality. It is geared to responding to pressing urgency. All decisions are short-term, survival-based. Everything else has to be deferred until later. That sounds reasonable—but what if your later is more of the same? Another crisis lurking, imminent, waiting its turn. That is not how life is to be lived—it is merely endurance.

Worse than the ceaseless struggle is the sense of being out of control. "Control"—the word flirts with us. We want it and can't have it. We resent the things and people who we feel control us. We dream of being or getting in control some day. It both beckons and eludes us.

The control we desire (to control the forces which govern us) is an illusion. Yet we do have control, although it seems so puny—the ability to control ourselves. It arises in each small choice, each word, each act. Do we take the little extra effort, which can never be justified, to be kind, helpful, encouraging, patient—

not just to others but to one's self? In each such sincere gesture we create a pocket of peace. To the extent we create it we can control it. We've received a reprieve from the battlefront. We've won a battle, and the prize is a moment of self-control.

Chapter 7

Bridge Mix
Lunchbox Notes

One day when my son Ross was a Junior in high school he asked me to pack him a lunch for school. Feeling maternal, I also wrote him a note and tucked it inside. That evening he commented that he would like me to keep packing him lunches—but only if there would be notes, too. Over the next few months I packed lunches and wrote the notes which follow. It turned out to be a good experience for both of us.

I would think of things to share while making the sandwiches, hoping to capture them fresh before he raced out the door. He would talk to me in the evening about his reactions and what they made him think about. Apparently, he shared them with some of his classmates, often leading to lively discussions. I offer them here as mental snackfood, a little something to nibble on.

To the Guy with His Eyes Filled with Wonder,

The heart sees more than the head. But when the two can learn to see/work together, you see/know it all. They were designed to be allies.

Life is too short to spend it:

Collecting grievances

Writing people off

Running in circles

Keeping score

Sending dirty looks

Reliving regrets

Planning revenge

Evading responsibility

There is always *enough* time. The trick is in being in control of how it is spent and seeing that it brings a "return." Each day provides a fresh supply and nobody gets any more than anyone else. But just look at what some people can do with it!

To the Late Night Scholar,

You are capable of more than you realize. Occasionally, under pressure, we "rise to the occasion" and discover our true ability. Then why do we so willingly sink back into the usual routine behaviors when the pressure is over? Anyone who solves that puzzle can tap those forces for accomplishing any goal desired.

Always trust the wee small voice that says, "I can find a better way to do this." It will keep your life fresh, creative and fun.

You can tell where you are by how you feel about the word "enough." If you think there is not enough, YOU'RE focusing on what is missing. There REALLY is enough. To see it, you need to shift to the mindset of abundance and possibilities. Then you can appreciate what is ALREADY available. From there you help things grow.

Youth is the time to dream the grand dream—to view what is possible. The purpose of education is to provide the skills needed to reach those dreams. Instead, educators have made them match by stifling and reducing the goal.

Every person, no matter how briefly they live or what they attain, changes the equation of the universe.

To The Squeaky Bow,

The hardest thing to do in life is develop the ability to trust yourself NO MATTER WHAT. Surely, you hope, there must be someone or something "out there" who is reliable. NO! Though you may feel you lack answers or ability, YOU are the most reliable "rock" in your world. Find the part of yourself inside that is solid and trustworthy. Value it, encourage it. Then avoid doing anything that doesn't relate to your anchor.

Fun isn't something that happens TO you. Give yourself permission to find fun in whatever you are doing.

Treasure this moment.

It is the best you will get.

Make your mark upon it.

As it makes its mark upon you.

Every activity you do is an opportunity to be original. The more routine the task the more the challenge, since finding new ways to do familiar activities is hard to do. You have to both break the tendency to think "It's the way I do it" and disrupt the physical habit. But any activity can be FUN and NEW when you constantly look for fresh non-habitual ways to do it.

We create our outlook on events by labeling them: "This is FUN;" "I'm having a BAD DAY." In truth, it's a series of events, but once they are "named" they are judged together and we relate to our "name" rather than the direct one-at-a-time experiences. Life is more fully (and more accurately) lived without such labels. It's also true for people and avoids stereotyping.

To the Scholarmeister,

There is a rhythm to the flow of events. Though they may appear random, they are not. There is always a pattern which can be discerned in the TIMING. Learn to read it and correspond to it. Then your efforts will encounter minimal resistance and frequent rewards. Go with the flow.

To an Intrepid Trooper,

Once in a while we surprise ourselves. We see an answer that is obvious, simple and elegant. Then there is a temptation to say "Why didn't I see it before?" or "Anyone could see it." NOT TRUE. You have lived with a notion or problem to the point that both you and the notion have been changed. The discovery of an answer is the signal of the growth.

My Trusty Trooper,

Even when someone does not "understand" us, we can gain from the exchange. We learn more about what WE mean and the effort to transmit the message clarifies our own thinking. We may even succeed in persuading ourselves with a deeper understanding of what was meant—and that's effective communication: FROM yourself, TO yourself.

Rossonavich,

Stupidity is the inability to learn from mistakes. Mistakes are your friends because they prod you to grow. Never curse that you made an error, but rather ask: "What can this teach me?" "Where is my invalid assumption?" When you can find a way to USE mistakes you welcome them.

Life is just a series of opportunities to do *your* best. The measure of your worth is in the degree of effort you deliver. The outcome, though important, is secondary.

Time management is nothing more than eliminating the distractions and low-priority time wasters that creep in. Unless you have established what is important and vital ALREADY, you will be unable to see what experiences are relevant to YOUR aims and discard the rest. Many demands on our time are urgent, yet not important. Don't be at the mercy of demands that don't further your goals and values, or you'll never get where you want to be.

Chessmaster,

There are short-term goals, mid-term goals and long-range goals. Long-range goals may take a long time, but they influence EVERY decision along the way. Unless you have a worthy long-range vision you will tend to drift and let the short-term answer or quick fix dictate your choices. It is less important what the long-range goals are than the fact that you have them.

The urge for security makes you define and seek a comfort zone. Then you do your darnedest not to get shoved out of it. Every significant accomplishment or lesson I've achieved has come by violating my urge to be secure. Most people cluster around the comfort zone—leaving you an open field in which to operate.

Beware the Siren's call of SECURITY.

Never trust anyone who thinks you should rely on them instead of yourself. Your function in life is to use your special combination of talents and limitations to achieve YOUR heart's desire. Figuring out how to do that takes a lifetime—your lifetime. No one can do it for you.

Take a lesson from quantum physics. When you look at something your attention or observation changes it. What you choose to notice in the people and events going on around you alters what occurs— even before you DECIDE what response you will make. Never underestimate the power of noticing.

Friendship is a special bond, partly with another person and partly with yourself. A friend is someone who lets you be "yourself" in their presence. And as they LIKE you, you like yourself better, too. That's why friends are so special and rare. You are both more complete whenever you touch.

The Goodie Gnome Says:

Forget about trying to figure out what you're going to do or be "when you grow up." Instead, find things you already do or know about that make you feel most alive. Look for more of those experiences and become more skilled there. You may not end up with that as a career, but you're already learning what your future role should FEEL LIKE. Remember, if you LOVE what you're doing, it doesn't seem like WORK.

Truth is not something cold and permanent. We each define what we think to be true. Then as we attempt to live with those truths, we discover they do not serve us well. Behind them are deeper more reliable levels of truth. You shall know the truth and the truth shall make you grow—and eventually free.

My Son,

Don't ever be so confident of success, so sure you have accomplished your goals that you step on someone "in the way." It is in little gestures at the moment of accomplishment that we reveal our values and priorities. That small inconvenience is in reality the final, yet most revealing test. As you accomplish great victories, "Don't kick the dog."

Everyone you speak to is telling you in many ways what they want to hear from you. When you start to respond to THOSE messages you will begin to know about communication.

My Young-un,

Whenever fear strikes, it has the effect of making us limit the choices that we think are available. We are unable to do our best thinking right at the time we need it most. Hint—you have more to fear from your own contracted and rigid brain at those times than from what you first feared. Refuse to "choose" at such times when you experience your greatest vulnerability.

To My Sidekick,

Sometimes things do not seem worth doing—and besides, who would notice? Our integrity grows when we do "our best" rather than simply slide along. Self-esteem without integrity is a fraud. The result or outcome does not determine the worth of the effort. But the degree of effort determines the worth of the person (besides, you'll know).

Boredom is a matter of choice. What is (or isn't) going on around us does not determine whether events are exciting. Boredom is an inability to be interested in an interesting world. It is about our outlook, not the view.

Sharing magnifies what we feel, what we experience. We are not solitary. When we share what occurs in our lives, we weave ourselves together—not just with those present, but with humanity.

Keep your mind open and your fly zipped.

There is the "letter of the law." There is the "spirit of the law." Now there is the "fun of the law." Don't be AGAINST order and social structure but find ways to PLAY with the rules, with restrictions. Find the fun of not being subservient to them. Bend them to YOUR BIGGER VISION.

"All growth is painful." (Max Brand)

But life without growth is also painful. Pain has a message: "learn—adapt—mature." In that sense pain is a helper, a prod. After you see that, you are glad for the experiences that nudged you to advance.

The advantage that young people have over everyone else is their certainty that they are invulnerable, that they can beat the odds. In this, youth is CORRECT. The ability to storm the established and defined "givens" is the force that can, indeed, move mountains. Unfortunately, such unstoppable power is seldom placed in service to a worthy goal. Instead, it becomes another world-moving opportunity frittered away.

Kittenhandler,

Having 5 fluffy kittens shows that curiosity can be a full-time activity. If you treat every day and everything you encounter as new, they will never fail to open, hitherto unseen doors for you. The world is your playground—if you bring the innocence and curiosity of a kitten.

Learn something every day that you don't think you need to know. Then watch and see how quickly it comes in handy.

What do you daydream about? Be honest. Would you want your dream life to be your real life? Or is it just an escape from your life? Every great achievement started as a dream. Turn your notions into motions. *Create your dream!*

Words can give you power! Powerful words provide impact on your thinking and talking. Declare war on puny, limp, bland words such as: nice, good, bad, fine, or O.K. Replace them with potent, precise, dramatic words.

Most of your education occurs outside the classroom. Your true teachers are the ones who you learn the most from. Who really is your teacher? Is what you're learning good for you?

Pretend you won the lottery and had all the money you would ever need. How would you spend your time—every day, the rest of your life? Now find a career or an industry that lets you do the same thing every day.

Be constantly prepared to be surprised! There is always more going on than you are noticing; but if you're still, alert and watch out of the corner of your eye, you'll catch the tiny signals. Objects can speak to you when you get on their wavelength.

You were born perfect with a destiny beyond your imagination. Go *claim* it.

Conclusion

BonBons
The Recipe

A BonBon is created when truth is pushed through a lens (an experience, a point of view, a personality), which then yields an insight. In some way, each of them carries the messages:

Life is designed to bring out the best in you.

Be aware; be alive; be alert.

Find the lesson and grow.

There is a powerful message to be found in every event, every encounter.

Enjoy whatever you do and, if possible, share it.

People matter; kindness helps.

You have more power and choices available than you realize or use.

Resist your familiar and habitual reactions; try new responses.

Life is precious; so are you.

Self-discovery is the most challenging frontier, and there is never an end to it.

Be grateful for the obstacles you encounter; use them to grow.

There are many ways to see things and to respond to them; don't limit yourself.

Pursue and enjoy the unexpected.

Be an active force in your own life.

Seek and accept your own wisdom.

Truth becomes more real and complete for you each time you encounter it and respond to it.

Find the fun, the humor inherent in everything that comes your way.

What you *DO* is more important than what you think (though it reveals and reflects what you think).

Challenge yourself to stay creative and fresh.

Experience the abundance of available energy whenever you add BonBons to your daily diet. You can make some for yourself from the ingredients available to you in your own life. Your unique identity adds an additional flavor, and you receive something even better than truth—YOUR OWN TRUTH. Remember, you can make a BonBon every time you push truth through your unique lens of awareness, through your identity, and discover an insight. Such insights can nourish and enliven you.

Bon Appetit!

The box will never be empty, and neither will your life!

Titles—In Alphabetical Order

FREE! BonBon Newsletter

Don't think of this as the end of the book, think of it as the "beginning of a beautiful friendship." There are more BonBons to come, and other treasures, too. Off the Page Press publishes a newsletter for readers like you. It includes unpublished BonBons, contributions from readers and other amusing and useful nuggets. We'd like to offer the newsletter to you for FREE.

Note to the reader from Lynella

Everything contained in this book was cooked up by me and is offered to you with warm affection. It has been my most sincere desire that you would find something to enjoy, to use, to share, to live by. I do not envision a one-way message. If you have a response or comment, please share it with me. If you have a favorite piece, or if a BonBon has improved your life, I'd like to know.

Lynella Grant, The Problem D'Solver™
c/o Off the Page Press
P.O. Box 1269
Scottsdale, AZ 85251

Electronic address: Frivel@aol.com

Here's all you have to do

Send a letter or postcard to Off the Page Press with your name, address and phone number, or email to Frivel@aol.com. You're invited to contribute to the newsletter.

Announcing:
BonBon Contest

A BonBon is created when truth is pushed through a unique point of view and yields an insight. The range of topics is infinite, as diverse as human life. Now you can share your own BonBons. You are invited to submit your BonBons in an annual contest. The following categories will each have two $100 winners: Values, Relationships, Feelings, Everyday Life, Nature.

1. Each contribution should be your own creation. If it has been previously published, please identify the date and publication.

2. Each entry must be between 200 and 800 words. Originality and humor are encouraged. Poetry is acceptable, if appropriate.

3. The deadline for receipt of entries is December 31 for each year's contest, starting in 1996.

4. No entries will be returned without an SASE (self-addressed, stamped envelope). All published entries become the property of Off the Page Press.

5. Every entry must show your name, address, phone number and date of submission.

6. Decision of the judges is final.

Send entries or queries to:
BonBon Contest
P.O. Box 1269
Scottsdale, AZ 85251

Did you borrow this book? Want a copy of your own?
Need a great gift for a friend or loved one?

Order Form

Yes, I want a personal copy of this book. Send _____ copies of *BonBons to Sweeten Your Daily Life, Wisdom that Works!* for $12.00 each, $55 for six, or $88.00 for 12.

Please add $3.00 per order for shipping and handling.

Arizona residents include 7% sales tax.

Foreign orders must be accompanied by a postal money order in U.S. funds.

Send check or credit card information to:

Off the Page Press, P.O. Box 1296, Scottsdale, AZ 85251

Name_____Phone _____

Address_____

City_____ State_____ Zip_____

☐ Here's my check/money order for $_____
(including $3.00 per order for shipping and handling).

☐ I prefer to use a credit card. Please bill my:

☐ VISA   ☐ MasterCard   ☐ American Express

Account Number _ _ _ _ _ _ _ _ _ _ _ _ _ _ _

Expiration Date_____Signature_____

*Contact Off the Page Press for
the discount rate for larger orders.*